Artificial Intelligence in Psychology

Explorations in Cognitive Science
Margaret A. Boden, general editor

Artificial Intelligence in Psychology

Interdisciplinary Essays

Margaret A. Boden

A Bradford Book

The MIT Press
Cambridge, Massachusetts
London, England

Second printing, 1989

This book was printed and bound by Halliday Lithograph in the
United States of America.

Library of Congress Cataloging-in-Publication Data

Boden, Margaret A.
    Artificial intelligence in psychology: interdisciplinary essays/
Margaret A. Boden.

    p. cm.—(Explorations in cognitive science)
    Consists of reprints from various sources with minor revisions.
    "A Bradford Book."
    Bibliography: p.
    Includes index.
    ISBN 0–262–02285–0. — ISBN 0–262–52140–7 (soft)
    1. Cognition—Data processing.   2. Artificial intelligence.
3. Cognitive science.   I. Title.   II. Series.
    [DNLM: 1. Artificial Intelligence—collected works.
2. Psychology—collected works.   BF 38 B666a]
BF311.B575   1989
153'.028'563—dc19
DNLM/DLC
for Library of Congress   88-38485
                                                                      CIP

For Margaret McGowan

Contents

Preface

The papers collected here — all, bar one, written between 1982 and 1988 — explore various aspects of the relevance of artificial intelligence to psychology.

Because they focus on differing specifics under this general unifying theme, they originally appeared in a wide range of sources and were addressed to distinct audiences. Some are drawn from professional journals: of philosophy, of psychology, and of biology. Of the two written for a non-academic audience, one appeared in the non-specialist journal of the New York Academy of Sciences, the other in a lecture-series organized by the Institute of Contemporary Arts (London). A few were composed for deliberately interdisciplinary publications: volumes on education, on scientific theory, and on adaptation in ill-defined systems. And one is an extract from a longer chapter in my recent monograph, *Computer Models of Mind: Computational Approaches in Theoretical Psychology* [Boden, 1988]. The only paper written before 1982 (Chapter 5) dates from 1970, and was included also in my previous collection, *Minds and Mechanisms* [Boden, 1981a].

The *Introduction* (Chapter 1) is newly written for this volume, and provides a general philosophical context for the essays that follow. It includes a brief sketch and discussion of connectionism, a recent development mentioned in several chapters (especially Chapter 4) which is sometimes said — wrongly — to show that artificial intelligence is psychologically irrelevant.

I have made only minor textual revisions to the papers themselves. Contextual references to the original sources have been removed; two brief insertions have been added to Chapter 5, and some long paragraphs divided; Chapter 7 is a conflation of two texts; and a few references have been included in the two non-academic papers (Chapter 2 and 4). Also, I have up-dated the publication details throughout; so the date identifying a bibliographical item may be later than the initial publication-date of the chapter in which it is cited.

Brighton, January 1988

Acknowledgments

I am grateful to Robert Bolick for his advice on the compilation of these essays. Also, I thank the relevant publishers for permission to reprint the following papers: *Chapter 2:* Fashions of Mind (first published as "In Search of Unicorns"), *The Sciences,* New York Academy of Sciences, 23: No. 5 (1983), 18-21; *Chapter 3:* Is Computational Psychology Constructivist? *Archives de Psychologie* (Geneva), 53 (1985), 103-112; *Chapter 4:* Does Artificial Intelligence Need Artificial Brains? In S. Rose & L. Appignanesi (eds.), *Science and Beyond* (ICA Lectures). Oxford: Blackwell, 1986. Pp. 103-114; *Chapter 5:* Intentionality and Physical Systems, *Philosophy of Science,* 37 (1970), 200-214; *Chapter 6:* Escaping from the Chinese Room. Part of Chapter 8 of M. A. Boden, *Computer Models of Mind: Computational Approaches in Theoretical Psychology.* Cambridge: Cambridge University Press, 1988. Pp. 238-251; *Chapter 7:* This chapter comprises the whole of "Is Equilibration Important? — A View from Artificial Intelligence," *British Journal of Psychology,* 73 (1982) 165-173, and part of "Failure is Not the Spur," first published in O. G. Selfridge, M. A. Arbib, & E. L. Rissland (eds.), *Adaptive Control in Ill-Defined Systems.* New York: Plenum, 1984. Pp. 305-316; *Chapter 8:* Artificial Intelligence and Biological Intelligence. *Human Evolution* (in press). Also in H. J. Jerison & I. L. Jerison (eds.), *The Evolutionary Biology of Intelligence.* Berlin: Springer-Verlag (in press); *Chapter 9:* The Educational Implications of Artificial Intelligence. In W. Maxwell (ed.), *Thinking: The Expanding Frontier.* Philadelphia: Franklin Institute Press, 1983. Pp. 227-236.

Artificial Intelligence in Psychology

I was well aware that the mechanical generalizations I had organized contained within them much more than I had leisure to study, and some things which will probably remain unproductive to a far distant day.

Charles Babbage
Ninth Bridgwater Treatise, 1837

Chapter 1

Introduction

Countess Lovelace was notorious in her lifetime as the daughter of the scandalous Lord Byron, the wife of the progressive Earl of Lovelace, and the champion of the eccentric engineer Charles Babbage. A century later, her fame is due to friend rather than to family. She is remembered primarily as Babbage's amanuensis, as a ghost-writer capable of appreciating the broader implications (if not all the mathematical details [Stein, 1985]) of his work. For Babbage's mid-nineteenth century designs of "Analytical Engines" specified precursors of the machines now being used in computer science [Hyman, 1982].

Psychologists, in particular, recall Ada Lovelace's clear expression of the insight that a machine—of a type essentially comparable to a digital computer—"might act upon other things besides numbers *were objects found whose mutual fundamental relations could be expressed by those of the abstract science of operations, and which should also be susceptible of adaptations to the action of the operating notation and mechanism of the engine.*"

For many theoretical psychologists today believe that the relevant "abstract science of operations" is that branch of computer science known as artificial intelligence (AI), for whose "engines" computer programs provide the "operating notation". And they claim that those "other things" of which the Countess spoke could in principle include not only (as she herself suggested) the composition of "elaborate and scientific pieces of music of any degree of complexity or extent" but also many other—some would say, all other—phenomena generated by the human mind. Accordingly, they believe that AI-concepts can contribute to the substantive content of theories about human (and animal) psychology, and that the coherence and implications of these theories can be rigorously tested if they are expressed as computer programs to be run on functioning machines. Much as Lady Lovelace claimed that Babbage's Analytical Engine "*weaves algebraic patterns* just as the Jacquard-loom weaves flowers and leaves", so her modern admirers see the mind's rich tapestry as a mass of psychological patterns woven from computational thread.

In short, psychologists inspired by AI-ideas ("computational" psychologists) assume that Ada Lovelace was essentially correct. This assumption underlies the three broad respects in which all such psychologists agree.

They adopt a functionalist approach to the mind, defining mental states in terms of their causal effects (on other mental states and behaviour) and seeking to identify mental processes with specific effective procedures. They see the mind as a representational system, psychology being the study of the various computational processes whereby mental representations are constructed, organized, interpreted, and transformed. And third, they approach neuroscience with computational questions in mind, asking what sorts of logical operations or functional relations are embodied in the brain (rather than which brain-cells do the embodying, and how their physiology makes this embodiment possible).

There are many disagreements, however, about precisely how various psychological phenomena are to be explained in computational terms. Some disputes, occurring against a considerable background of shared theoretical analysis, can be resolved by testing in organisms and/or artefacts; many arguments about the details of low-level vision, or 2D-to-3D mapping, can be so settled. Others involve controversy about the basic theoretical categories appropriate to a certain domain; for instance, theories and computer models of parsing do not all rely on the same underlying grammar. There are "internal" differences, too, over the potential scope of a computational science of the mind: emotions, motivation, belief—and even cryptarithmetic—have each been despaired of by someone of this persuasion (not to mention psychologists of other, non-computational, persuasions).

In general, researchers disagree about which particular AI concepts, and which of the various computer-modelling methodologies, are likely to be the most useful from the psychologist's point of view.

Among the things about which computational psychologists—and AI- workers too—differ among themselves is the issue of just how important is the brain's particular way of embodying the mind. Can thought and action be generated only by systems whose basic architecture is brainlike, involving parallel-processing within networks of associated cells? Must the physical properties and organization of any thinking machine, whether in Malibu or on Mars, be fundamentally like the brain? Or could a creature (whether organism or artefact) enjoy comparable psychological powers embodied in an utterly different manner?

Lady Lovelace surmised that some such powers could be attributed not only to biological creatures, but to technological ones too. However, ideas about the potential of technology cannot be demonstrated in practice until the requisite technology exists. Babbage's most ambitious Analytical Engines never left the drawing-board, for even his creative expertise in precision-tooling could not build functional moving-part engines to his own abstract specifications. Likewise, Alan Turing a century later described an abstract machine (a "universal Turing machine") capable of computing *any* computable function—but he could not (yet) build a useful approximation to it. Such approximations were soon to be built, however (by Turing himself, among others), taking advantage of mid-twentieth century developments in electronics. (Actual machines can at best approximate a universal Turing machine, because this mathematically-defined computational system stores its symbols on an infinite tape.)

Today, the digital computer based on John von Neumann's designs of the 1940's—and fundamentally similar in several ways to Babbage's plans for Analytical Engines (the first of which was drafted over a century earlier)—is a familiar dimension of life in industrialized countries. Artificial intelligence research—indeed, computer science in general—has been done almost without exception on digital computers.

This is true not only of technological projects, but of computer simulations of mental processes too. Virtually all the computer models regarded by psychologists as relevant to mental life are implemented on von Neumann machines. Moreover, many of the theories propounded by computational psychologists show the conceptual influence of this particular technology. For computational concepts drawn from artificial intelligence were developed in the context of research using the von Neumann machine, with its strictly serial processing of precisely-locatable binary symbols. Such concepts and associated theories may be termed formalist, since they assume that *computation* and *representation* necessarily involve symbol-manipulation defined in terms of formal rules.

However, some psychological theories developed within the computationalist persuasion posit mental processes of a type better-suited to "engines" of a very different kind: namely, brains. From the very earliest days of the digital computer, some people used them to simulate machines engaged in the parallel processing of probabilistic, and continuously varying, information. Now, the digital computer is increasingly used in this way, to model brain-like, "connectionist", information-processing systems whose computational properties differ significantly from those of more familiar sorts of programs.

For example, various forms of "parallel distributed processing" (PDP) systems are being investigated in which a pattern, concept, or representation is not stored at any particular (addressable) place in the machine but in an entire network of continually interacting computational units [Rumelhart & McClelland, 1986a]. The units either reinforce or inhibit their neighbours' activity—much as interconnected nerve-cells do. The connections between the units can be (though as yet rarely are) implemented as hardwired links, or they can be programmed (simulated on a von Neumann machine). In either case, the behaviour of the system as a whole emerges from the myriad excitatory and inhibitory connections between its constituent units.

Such a system may be broadly compared with a classroom full of children, each of whom chatters continuously with her neighbours about some detail relevant to the interpretation, or decision, which the class is trying to achieve. A child's current opinion can be directly reinforced or inhibited by the messages she receives from her immediate neighbours. But because her neighbours are communicating directly with children in other desks, who in turn are talking to peers in yet more distant places, her opinion can be indirectly affected by every child in the room who has something relevant to say. Each child repeatedly modifies her opinion in the light of what her neighbours say (the desks are arranged so that children holding opinions on the same topic, or on closely relevant topics, are seated near to each other). Eventually, all the children's (confidently-held) opinions come to be mutually consistent. The final interpretation or decision is not made by any one child (there is no "class captain", sitting at an identifiable desk) but by the entire collectivity, being embodied as the overall pattern of mutually-consistent mini-opinions held (with high confidence) within the classroom.

The resultant decision is thus due to the *parallel processing* (all the children chatter simultaneously) of *localized computations* (each child speaks to, and is directly influenced by, only her immediate neighbours), and is *distributed* across the whole system (as an internally consistent set of mini-decisions made by all the children).

This broad analogy can be refined by distinguishing various types of classroom [Boden, 1988, chs. 3 & 7]. For instance, each child may be able to say only "yes" or "no"; or she may be able to differentiate varying degrees of "maybe". Again, each child may always pronounce only opinions consistent with the evidence available to her; or she may sometimes venture an opinion unrelated to the evidence, a sort of random epistemic hiccup. (Nerve cells "hiccup" too: the stochastic nature of neuronal activity has been recognized since the 1950's [Burns, 1968]). The children may have overlapping interests, in that they are sensitive to partially-shared evidence; or they may not. (Many biological cells share evidence: thus retinal cells have overlapping receptive fields.) And the children's individual judgments may be more, or less, finely tuned. (A neurone's range of inputs may be large or small; the receptive fields of retinal cells are not near-approximations to points, but have an appreciable size.)

Diverse classrooms are comparable with connectionist systems having distinct computational properties—some of which may be surprising. Thus a roomful of hiccupping children is in principle (though not in practice) guaranteed to reach the right decision, whereas a class of children who always stick closely to the evidence is not [Hinton & Sejnowski, 1986]. (So stochastic neural activity in the brain may not be "botched" biological engineering, but may convey an evolutionary advantage.) And a decision which involves fine discriminations on several dimensions need not be (though in principle—and sometimes in practice—it can be) carried out by a group of children each of whom is sensitive to only one possible value of only one dimension. Indeed, a complex decision may be more efficiently reached by a smaller classroom containing not very discriminating children (whose interests overlap) than by a much larger classroom of children capable of very finely-tuned individual judgments (each of whom minds only her own business) [Hinton, 1981] . (So the fact that retinal receptors do not respond to stimulus-areas as small as possible may be a strength rather than a weakness.)

Some current investigations of brain-like computational systems are purely abstract or mathematical, as was the later work of Babbage (on Analytical Engines) and the early work of Turing (on universal Turing machines). It is mathematical analysis which proves, for example, that a class of hiccupping children (a "Boltzmann machine") is guaranteed to reach the optimal interpretation eventually. However, "eventually"—as the mathematician understands it—may be a very long, perhaps even an infinite, time. In practice, Boltzmann machines can be relied on to reach the correct solution only if there is negligible irrelevant information, or noise. Being interested in how finite systems (organisms or computer models) behave in real time, the psychologist needs to know to what extent abstract mathematical analyses of system-competence are practically useful descriptions of actual system-performance. Moreover, an abstract competence-analysis is not always available.

Accordingly, many studies of connectionist computational systems involve empirical explorations of the properties of real "engines". At present, these engines can only be digital computers, programmed to simulate associative networks. But associative hardware of several kinds is now being developed, to serve both technological and theoretical purposes [e.g. Hillis, 1985].

By the turn of the century, the AI-researcher's laboratory will house not only von Neumann computers but various purpose-built parallel machines as well. Some of these, perhaps, may be made not of silicon but of neuroprotein. And their "abstract science of operations" may resemble the equations of thermodynamics (for example) more than the principles of computer science as we know them today. Much as Lady Ada herself could not foresee all the applications of Babbage's visionary ideas, so we cannot know just which mental processes will or will not be modelled when various sorts of associative hardware are routinely available.

Nor do we have an answer with respect to von Neumann architecture, for we cannot specify what computational tasks might actually be effected by such machines. Certainly, digital computers are approximations to universal Turing machines, which can compute any computable function. But a proof that a task could in principle be performed by a certain type of computational system (whether digital computer or Boltzmann machine) does not guarantee that it can be successfully tackled by any such system in practice. With respect both to technological artificial intelligence and to AI-influenced psychology, the potential of digital computers has not yet been exhausted and the exploration of connectionist systems has only just begun.

Nevertheless, AI-workers and psychologists alike can already ask some relevant theoretical questions. Some of these concern the relevance of AI-ideas to specific topics, which are of course innumerable (those discussed below include ethology, education, and equilibration). But of those questions which are more general in nature, five broad classes may be distinguished. These deal respectively with: (1) abstract task-analysis; (2) analysis and (3) testing of various computer-models (perhaps comparing their performance with the behaviour of human—and animal—subjects); (4) the relations between formalist and connectionist approaches within computational psychology; and (5) the nature of *computation* as such, and its relevance to *representation* and *understanding* .

The *first* class of questions concerns the computations which must be performed by any system (brainlike or not) capable of performing a certain task. An answer will be relevant to any psychological theory, or computer model, of the task concerned. Competence-analyses have no necessary connection with computational psychology, and may be produced by researchers not wedded to this approach (Chomsky's grammar was not developed by computer modelling). But because of the quasi-mathematical nature of competence analysis, someone engaged in this pursuit is likely to have some sympathy for the computational approach. Moreover, successful task-analyses will be useful for both traditionalist and "non-von" (parallelist) computer modelling. So insights originally developed and/or incorporated within the formalist tradition are now being applied within the connectionist approach. For example, the notion of gradient space—first formulated within the formalist programme of "scene analysis", whose task was to interpret line-drawings in three-dimensional terms [Mackworth, 1973, 1983]—has been used within parallel-processing theories of low-level vision [Marr, 1982].

A large proportion of work in computational psychology addresses the *second* and *third* types of question, in that it uses both abstract argument and empirical testing of computer models (often backed up by observation of human behaviour) to study the varying computational and representational properties of distinct types of system. For instance, one can investigate various methods of knowledge-representation (semantic nets, scripts, frames, production systems, and so on) in formalist computer models—and in human subjects too. Or one can analyse and explore models, often incorporating similar theoretical ideas, based on diverse forms of connectionism (different sorts of classroom).

The computational advantage of epistemic hiccupping, and the relative efficiency of sets of coarsely-tuned and overlapping discriminators, are examples of surprising abstract results in this area. Surprising empirical results (unexpected computer-performance), likewise, are found in both formalist and connectionist models. One formalist example is a filtering algorithm for economizing on computation, which turned out to be far better at avoiding the combinatorial explosion than its programmer had foreseen [Waltz, 1975; Boden, 1987, pp. 222-226]. A connectionist example is a computer model which learns the past tense of English verbs by "hearing" them, and whose learning-pattern shows temporal changes closely comparable to those observed in infant speech [Rumelhart & McClelland, 1986b]. Although its performance is describable by the rules of English past- tense morphology, these rules are neither programmed into it nor explicitly represented in it as a result of its learning. Rather, it develops associative equilibrium-patterns which cause the system to behave *as though* it were following rules of a type which could be (and often are) made explicit in a von Neumann machine. (What is "surprising" of course depends on one's prior knowledge: someone who understands the general principles of the past-tense learner could predict some, though not all, of the performance-patterns observed.)

As for the relations between formalist and connectionist approaches in artificial intelligence, this *fourth* question can take various forms. One can ask, for instance, whether some specific psychological phenomena, as opposed to others, are better understood (and modelled) in formalist or in connectionist terms. The current consensus is that connectionist theory is better-suited to the understanding of pattern-matching (including analogy) and content-addressable memory. Not only can connectionist systems speedily perform complex pattern-recognition tasks which formalist systems cannot, but their performance shows graceful degradation—it gets gradually worse with increasing noise, as the human's does—where formalist models would give utterly inappropriate responses. (Even so, many of the theoretical insights contributing to connectionist models of pattern-matching originated in a formalist context.) By contrast, formalist models seem better-suited to the understanding of certain sorts of reasoning, such as cryptarithmetic. Indeed, a connectionist pattern-matcher may have to simulate a von Neumann machine in order to do arithmetic [Rumelhart, Smolensky, McClelland, & Hinton, 1986].

Another way of putting the fourth question is to ask whether connectionism is an example of artificial intelligence, or of computational psychology, at all. Are formalist and connectionist approaches close cousins, enjoying a friendly rivalry in a shared family-game? Or are they fundamentally alien contestants for the prize of understanding the mind?

Some critics of AI's influence on psychology describe recent parallelist models as a potentially "devastating" challenge to conventional computational psychology, and to conventional AI itself [Dreyfus & Dreyfus, in press]. Similarly, connectionist computer-modelers sometimes argue that ideas drawn from AI-work on von Neumann machines have fundamentally misled psychologists for the last quarter-century. Indeed, some connectionists describe their approach as "a radical departure from the symbolic paradigm", and assign it to "the sub-symbolic paradigm" instead [Smolensky, 1987, p.101].

However, the "radical departure" of connectionism is not the adoption of a radically incommensurable viewpoint, as would be required for it to constitute a distinct paradigm [Kuhn, 1962]. Rather, it is a change of emphasis with respect to some relatively basic ideas within the general computational approach. Both connectionist and non-connectionist forms of artificial intelligence and of computational psychology owe their origins to the same mid-century ideas about the brain's logical-computational potential [McCulloch & Pitts, 1943]. This seminal work not only led to pioneering connectionist research on neural nets [Rosenblatt, 1958, 1962] but also influenced von Neumann in his design of the digital computer. Moreover, many ideas about the computational structure of mental tasks that were originally developed within the von Neumann context have contributed to the design of parallel-processing systems.

It is hardly surprising, in view of these facts, that some leading connectionists insist that "it would be wrong to view distributed representations as an *alternative* to representational schemes like semantic networks or production systems that have been found useful in cognitive psychology and artificial intelligence" [Hinton, McClelland, & Rumelhart, 1986, p. 78; italics in original]. These researchers view PDP-networks rather as "one way of implementing these more abstract schemes in parallel networks", saying that connectionist networks provide powerful pattern-matching operations that can be regarded as "primitives" by psychologists considering higher-level theories implemented (if at all) in more traditional ways.

If computational psychology is a paradigm, then, connectionism should be included as a particular development within it. However, it might be better to avoid the term "paradigm" altogether in this context. A scientific paradigm is largely defined by a sociological criterion, according to which it enjoys the wide, and basically uncritical, acceptance of some entire scientific community. If the relevant community is psychologists at large, then computational psychology does not constitute a paradigm. Many more psychologists ignore, or even oppose, it than profess it (and some of these study those psychological phenomena to which one might expect the computational approach to be relevant, if it is relevant at all). Unless and until this fact changes, the term "paradigm" seems inapplicable purely on a sociological grounds.

One might attempt to drive a wedge between the two approaches by reference to the topic of our *fifth* question: the nature of computation, and of representation. The familiar (formalist) definition of "computation" applies *par excellence* to information-processing in von Neumann machines, which involves the serial application of explicitly stored formal-syntactic rules to explicit, and localizable, symbolic representations. But the information-processes within connectionist models are very different. Are non-sequential, cooperative, and equilibrium-seeking alterations of patterns-of-activity really computations? Are specifications of the progressive self-organization of a network of computational units really *algorithms* ? Are information-processing interdependencies that are implicit in the excitatory and inhibitory connections between units really *rules* ? Are widely-distributed excitation-patterns really embodiments of *symbols*—or even*representations* ? Or does connectionism imply—contrary to the basic assumptions of computational psychology—that there are no representations in the brain (no hardware-independent abstract descriptions), so no question of explaining cognition in terms of representations?

The formalist definition of computation, and of artificial intelligence and computational psychology too, is unnecessarily restrictive. Connectionist systems—like formalist ones—are concerned with information-processing. Formalists sometimes suggest that connectionist theories are concerned with implementation, with "the nervous system's instantiation" of psychological operations [Pylyshyn, 1984, p. 215]. But only if a connectionist system were intended as a neuroscientific model of specific neural circuitry and synaptic interactions would it be a model of implementation, as opposed to information-processing. And connectionist theories satisfy the general criteria of computationalism identified above—albeit in ways which differ from more traditional computer models.

Connectionist systems are not von Neumann machines, in which information-processing rules are explicitly coded within and accessed by the program. But they are designed so as to follow rigorous rules in passing from one state to another, and in seeking an equilibrium. These rules ensure that the patterns of excitation and inhibition in the system vary in a way which reflects significant informational constraints. Such rules are implicit in the system (being implemented as interconnections), and do not enable one to specify precisely "what will happen next" from moment to moment. But their function in determining information-processing justifies their being regarded as a (different) type of algorithm.

Likewise, by means of varying weights and excitation-states, "non-von" machines manipulate symbols—of an unusual kind. In so doing, they may be said to perform computations, for their passage from one symbolic state to another can be mapped onto logical-semantic relations of various kinds. Admittedly, their symbols are implemented very differently from those in a von Neumann computer, and (in an associative machine) are not hardware-independent in the same way. No individual unit implements any identifiable symbol or meaning, for meaningful representations exist only at the level of networks made up of many units. But such (distributed) representations, too, have properties that can be mapped onto abstract relationships of various kinds. And they, too, are able to mediate causal connections with the world, and with other representations and processes internal to the system itself.

The preceding paragraph presupposes a particular sort of answer to the fifth question (concerning the nature of computation). Specifically, it presupposes that meaning, symbolism, representation—and computation too—can be ascribed to a system in virtue of its having certain causal-information processes going on inside it. Although these processes may be physically implemented, they are not describable in physical terms. Accordingly, the question as to what sort of physical implementation they can have cannot be answered *a priori*. Clearly they can be embodied in the neuroprotein of human and animal brains; possibly, they can be embodied likewise in inorganic materials, such as metal and silicon. The behaviour of the system—above all, its "internal behaviour", describable in information-processing terms—determines whether it computes and understands, and what meanings or semantic contents are represented by it. To compute and to understand are fundamentally similar, which is why computational psychology could give us a science of the mind.

This claim is highly controversial. "Computation" is widely believed (even by many AI-workers and computational psychologists) to exclude semantics. The charge is often made that it therefore cannot possibly explain meaning, representation, or understanding—in a word, intentionality. Since the mind is a source of meanings, and the brain an embodiment of intentionality, theories couched in terms of computation simply cannot (on this view) account for human, or even animal, psychology.

The starting-point for this reasoned rejection of artificial intelligence—and therefore of computational psychology—as a route to the understanding of the mind is the formalist definition of computation (given above), which takes it to be the application of formal-syntactic rules to identifiable symbolic representations. To say that a rule is formal-syntactic is to say that it applies (or not) to the symbol concerned *only* as a function of the symbol's form. It follows (or so the argument goes) that the symbol's meaning—if indeed it has any—has nothing to do with the application of the rule. A system consisting of such rules, no matter how complex it may be, cannot thereby mean or understand anything: it cannot thereby enjoy intentionality. If it does understand anything, or embody any genuine representation having semantic content, it does so in virtue of some property other than the possession of symbol-manipulating rules. Since a computer program is nothing but a collection of formal-syntactic rules, computer models can never provide an adequate explanation of intentionality.

My response to this charge is that even the simplest computer program has properties which are essential to understanding (though this is not to say that computer programs can "understand" in anything like the familiar sense of the term). Since a program enables a computer to function in specific ways, it is not a mere formal calculus. Rather, it is the basis of a causal nexus of simple, and specifiable, information-processes which are at the same time both sufficiently like and sufficiently unlike the more complex processes involved in genuine understanding to provide an explanation of it [Boden, 1962]. In other words, computer programs provide computers with the beginnings of what in human minds we recognize as intentionality.

These somewhat cryptic remarks rebutting the formalist view of computation are elaborated in Chapter 6, below—and my response to the other questions outlined above is contained in the following papers. The essays concerned with the philosophical nature and the methodology of AI-influenced psychology in general comprise the first two-thirds of the book (which also includes some discussion of computational theories of vision). The later chapters discuss the application of computational ideas to development and creativity, to ethology, and to education.

Fashions of Mind (Chapter 2) provides an introductory sketch (written for a non-specialist audience) of the computational approach, set against the historical background of psychology in which confusingly diverse theoretical notions have waxed and waned over the years. This newest approach will surely develop and change, as our knowledge of the range of possible computational systems grows (recent work on connectionist systems is one seed of such future development). In particular, computational psychology will become increasingly integrated with neuroscience—whose detailed advance will itself draw significantly on computational insights. But unlike many past psychological fads, this new approach will not disappear. Its lasting contributions include an unprecedented standard of explanatory rigor, a conceptual framework capable of encompassing both observable behaviour and internal mental processes, and a theoretical acceptance of intentionality and of the various human phenomena grounded in it.

In the latter regard, AI-grounded psychology differs radically from behaviourism—which eschewed all mentalistic concepts. Whether computational psychologists have a philosophical *right* to use intentional concepts is controversial, as we have seen (in Chapter 6, I argue that they do). But since they do use them, and regard them as essential for the description and scientific understanding of human (and animal) minds, they are not open to the charge of dehumanization often, and correctly, made against behaviouristic theories.

In **Is Computational Psychology Constructivist?** (Chapter 3), I discuss the debate between perceptual psychologists of "rationalist" and "empiricist" persuasions. This debate is sometimes expressed in terms of an opposition between theories stressing "top-down" processes guided by learnt high-level schemas or representations, and theories relying on "bottom-up" processes of a more automatic, and unlearned, character. But there is a middle way, which (like theories of a more clearly "rationalist" character) is exemplified within computational psychology.

Computational research on low-level vision, for example, aims to explain how the seeing organism can use the input pattern of light as a source of information about the shapes, distances, sizes, and orientations of physical surfaces and objects. It does so without relying on high-level schemata (which are, however, brought in to explain other pervasive aspects of vision), and without appealing to sensorimotor learning as essential to the individuation of distinct physical objects. So far, so Gibsonian. But, unlike J. J. Gibson [1979], computational workers see low-level vision as a process in which representations on successive levels are actively (though unconsciously) constructed by the organism, employing innate mechanisms specifically evolved for the interpretation of 2D-input in 3D-terms.

The theory of visual representation discussed in Chapter 3 is due to D. C. Marr [1982], who saw it as a special case of a general approach to psychological theorizing—an approach he characterized in terms of three explanatory levels. The first level (called "computational" by Marr, even though it is *not* concerned with psychological *processes)* identifies the abstractly, or mathematically, defined computational task underlying the psychological domain in question. The second, algorithmic, level specifies, in information-processing terms, how the computation is actually effected in particular systems (which may have different ways of computing the same thing). And the third describes the hardware by means of which various systems (which may be very different) embody these information-processes. Put briefly: the first level identifies what is done, the second specifies how it is done, and the third describes what does it.

These distinctions are relevant to the question (raised above) whether an "engine" having psychological properties must be fundamentally brainlike—a question addressed in Chapter 4, **Does Artificial Intelligence Need Artificial Brains?** Specifically, this paper asks whether all intelligent engines must be made of the same stuff as the brain, whether they must be organized in much the same way as the brain is, and whether they must do much the same things as the brain does (even if they do them in a somewhat different way).

In other words, must a psychological system be made of neuroprotein? Must it be embodied as a parallel-processing, richly-associated, and largely dedicated information-processing machine? And must it address the same computational tasks as the brain does, and be subject to the same fundamental computational constraints? The answer given to the first of these questions (which is discussed in Chapter 6 also) is *"Perhaps not"*; the answer to the second is "In principle, *No*—but in practice, probably *Yes* "; and the answer to the third is "Largely, *Yes*.".

Although (as mentioned above) sizeable connectionist systems can in principle be simulated on a von Neumann architecture, they can in practice be embodied only on parallel-associative machines. As yet, evolution has produced such machines but manufacture has not. And it will be very many years—if ever—before manufacture (even of a "biological" kind) is able to produce parallel machines of a size and complexity comparable to brains. Even so, current work in connectionist computer-modelling is beginning to clarify what particular questions need to be asked about the parallel-processing properties of the brain, if we are to understand how our neuronal architecture provides us with computational powers of various kinds.

The various "classrooms" mentioned above are early examples of this type of work, focused on very general features of neural networks. A very recent example [Barrow, 1987] tackling a more specific neuroscientific question concerns those cells in the primary visual cortex which respond to edges or bars of light with particular orientations at specific locations in the visual field: the question is whether these highly selective cells could be developed through experience, by way of some adaptive mechanism, or whether each one must be innately "tuned" to its respective stimulus. The short answer is that a computational model of visual cortex can indeed be specified which, given visual images arising from surfaces in the natural world, could spontaneously self-organize as a set of cells with receptive fields like those actually found in mammalian brains. The longer answer would point out also that the (abstractly-specified) computational task which these cells are performing may be different from either of the alternatives currently debated by those concerned with visual neuroscience.

This reference to abstractly-defined computational tasks brings us to the third question discussed in Chapter 4: whether any intelligent engine must do what the brain does. A variety of current work is contributing to our understanding of the general computational constraints on *any* information-processing system facing a particular task. For instance, Marr's [1982] research on low-level vision (cited also in Chapter 3) is helping us to understand what "vision", or a specific visual task such as "stereopsis", really is—which will determine what any system must be able to do if it is to achieve visual stereopsis. Likewise, Chomsky aims to define what structures any system must be able to generate and interpret if it is to be able to use "language." Such enquiries are of an abstract, or mathematical, kind which does not necessarily require the construction of an actual computer model. (Correlatively, a theory of competence need not be accompanied by theory of performance.) Even if such a model turns out in practice to be a helpful tool for achieving these theoretical insights, it may be of a type very different from the brain. For example, it was pointed out above (and is exemplified in the history of computer vision sketched in Chapter 4) that work on "scene-analysis", done on von Neumann machines of the late 1960's, provided some useful insights into the abstract nature of "vision" as a computational task. In short, a machine very different from the brain may sometimes do what the brain does.

Whether an individual researcher has correctly identified the relevant computational task facing the brain (in a certain psychological domain) is always open to question. Thus certain aspects of Marr's analysis of real-world surfaces have been challenged (as noted in Chapter 3), and so has Chomsky's theory of syntactic structure [Gazdar, Klein, Pullum, & Sag, 1985]. It is sometimes controversial whether any identifiable computational task exists which underlies a given set of performances (such as mental arithmetic, attitude change, or the attribution of intentions). If it does not, then what may seem *prima facie* to be a unitary class of behaviours is in fact theoretically diverse. Most of the computationally-defined tasks performed by the brain (and by all engines with comparable powers of intelligence) are yet to be discovered, and they may not map neatly onto what are generally taken today to be the "natural kinds" of psychology. It remains true, however, that "what the brain is doing" is a crucial question for theoretical psychology and that the answer is independent of hardware.

The fifth and sixth chapters are both concerned with the challenge to computational psychology which (as remarked above) is presented by the phenomenon of intentionality. **Intentionality and Physical Systems** (Chapter 5) explains why intentionality has been thought by many philosophers to be inexplicable in terms of neurophysiology. It outlines those logical peculiarities of intentional contexts which have led some to deny the possibility of a unified science, in which psychological matters would be explained in basically mechanistic terms. And it agrees that intentional language and explanations cannot be reduced to, or translated by, statements about material embodiment.

It claims nevertheless that intentionality can be understood as a high-level property of certain sorts of material system, of which computers provide a readily intelligible (though very simple) example. And it argues that even psychosomatic phenomena, in which evidence for the causal influence of mind on body seems to be overwhelming, can be understood in computational terms. One could (for instance) simulate a hysterical paralysis in a robot, and the most persuasive descriptions and explanations of the robot's behaviour would show the very same logical peculiarities characteristic of intentional contexts in general. For example, its inability to move its hand would be attributable (like hysterical paralysis in human patients) to its concept of *hand,* and to some intention or programmed instruction defined in terms of that concept, rather than to the anatomical connections between its material equivalents of muscles, nerves, and bones.

It might be objected here that a description may be "persuasive" without being true. Certainly, *if* one chooses (as I do in Chapter 5) to use intentional language to describe such a robot, *then* one will attempt to use such language consistently—in which case the logical peculiarities pertaining to genuine intentionality will very likely be mirrored in speaking of the robot. (Were this not possible, at least to a significant degree, one would not be tempted to borrow intentional language in describing such cases.) The important question is whether one should allow oneself to be beguiled into using intentional language in the first place. Is it ever really appropriate to speak of a robot as having intentions or concepts? More generally, could one ever say truly that a computer program understands anything, in howsoever primitive a fashion?—If not, then computational psychology would seem to be doomed. For if one cannot correctly attribute understanding to computer programs then one cannot use theoretical concepts drawn from an AI-context to explain the understanding which is possessed by people.

This objection is rebutted in Chapter 6, **Escaping from the Chinese Room**. The Chinese room first figured in an ingenious thought-experiment designed by J. R. Searle [1980] to persuade people of the futility of using AI-concepts in psychology. Searle rejects "strong AI" (the notion that a sufficiently human-like computer program or robot would really understand, really see, really try . . .), and rejects likewise the claim that computational psychology could in principle explain human beings' ability to understand, to see, to try—in a word, their intentionality. Insofar as computational psychologists use computer programming merely to clarify the content and implications of their psychological theories, Searle is content. But he insists that the conceptual content of AI-ideas, or of computational theories based on them, cannot help psychologists to describe or explain mental processes as such, since minds possess intentionality whereas computers do not.

Searle's primary argument here takes for granted what was identified above as the "formalist" assumption: that AI-programs and computer models are purely formal-syntactic in nature. In rebuttal, I argue (in Chapter 6) that even the simplest program has some semantic properties, and that computational theories in psychology are therefore not purely formalist or essentially incapable of explaining meaning. (The fact that the semantic properties which are attributable to all computer programs are crudely simplistic in comparison with those possessed by minds, and that "understanding" in the familiar sense cannot be ascribed to any existing program, does not debar them from explaining human intentionality. For explanation always involves the assimilation of something to something else analogous to but not identical with it [Boden, 1962].) Searle's secondary argument is that it is intuitively obvious that whereas neuroprotein can generate intentionality, metal and silicon cannot. I reply that, insofar as the brain's ability to generate intentionality is intelligible to us at all—as opposed to being wholly counter-intuitive (how *could* that greyish mushy stuff possibly understand?)—it is intelligible only in information-processing terms which can be applied equally well to artificial systems such as computers.

Chapter 7 asks a question (**Is Equilibration Important?**) to which the answer, from a computational point of view, might seem to be an immediate—indeed, an impatient—*No!* For if (as claimed in Chapter 2) a prime characteristic of the influence of AI on psychology is its emphasis on rigour, one might expect the computational psychologist to dismiss such notoriously ill-defined concepts out of hand. In Chapter 7, however, I argue that Piaget's concept of equilibration, despite its undeniable vagueness, is of interest because it marks some deep questions—though provides no satisfactory answers—about development and creativity.

Coherent, progressive, and self-regulated change—which occurs in cognitive, biological, and social domains—is deeply problematic. Whether in the mind of the child, the thinking of the adult, or the morphology of the embryo, it appears to involve fundamental changes in organization and generative structures. These changes, which lead to the development of harmonious novelties rather than mere unfamiliar chaos, are not yet well understood. But various computational insights, detailed in Chapter 7, may be helpful in clarifying the relevant questions and suggesting some outline answers. The basic reason for this explanatory potential is that a computational approach takes seriously questions about the transformation of generative structures. Not all such transformations are radical, to be sure, still less in any interesting sense spontaneous. Even so, a computational approach promises to help us draw the general theoretical contours of development.

As for creativity, this is assumed by many people to be beyond the reach of AI-influenced psychology. Indeed, one of Countess Lovelace's comments on the Analytical Engine is widely regarded as an embarrassment to the computational approach, and is often cited by its opponents accordingly. She wrote that "The Analytical Engine has no pretensions whatever to *originate* anything. It can do [only] *whatever we know how to order it* to perform." Creativity, it seems, is utterly denied to computational engines—and to psychological theories based on computational roots. Chapter 7 argues, to the contrary, that creativity involves explorations and radical transformations of cognitive structures which are in principle intelligible in computational terms. These transformations enable a system to generate behaviour which is not only historically *new* (that is, it did not occur previously) but radically *novel*—that is, in some computationally intelligible sense, it *could not* have occurred before. Some examples of pertinent AI-research are mentioned in the chapter, though these are suggestive rather than definitive (also relevant is a recent computationally-based discussion of induction and discovery [Holland, Holyoak, Nisbett, & Thagard, 1986]). The central point, however, is that insofar as Piaget's concept of equilibration concerns the radical transformation of generative structures, it covers creativity as well as psychological and embryological development.

Biological considerations, of a very general kind, have already entered the discussion with respect to the necessity—or otherwise—of "brainlike" computers. In Chapter 8, the biological and evolutionary context of mind is even more visible. **Artificial**

Intelligence and Biological Intelligence suggests various ways in which specific AI-concepts and methods could be of use to ethologists seeking a systematic comparison of the psychology of different species.

Studies of planning, of low-level vision, of "naive physics", and of different forms of computation and representation are all relevant to the behaviour of many animals. Moreover, just as artificial intelligence forces us to confront the unsuspected complexity of apparently simple human abilities, so it points to the similarly unsuspected complexity of much animal behaviour. Recent experimental work in "cognitive ethology", for instance, has shown—what behaviourism would not admit—that a chimpanzee may be able to plan, to try, to cooperate, and to use symbols to communicate with another animal. An adequate ethology should tell us not only that they do these things, but also *how* they can do them. This question may not even be raised, still less answered, by ethologists using traditional methods. A computational approach, however, focuses on the information-processing mechanisms underlying such psychological powers (planning, intending, cooperating, communicating, and the like).

As well as aiding in the study of particular species, an AI-approach can help us explore—if not yet to map—the space of possible minds. It can suggest types of computation necessary or sufficient for certain capabilities, which accordingly might be available to species surprisingly low on the phylogenetic scale (for example, a computational analysis proves that the discrimination of an object's *shape* is not necessary for the computation of its *identity*). It can help clarify the distinction between tacit, or implicit, knowledge and explicit representation. It can significantly deepen the recent interest in "cognitive ethology" by indicating the often-unsuspected complexity of the mental processes attributed to animals. And it may throw some light on what one might mean by a "structural phenomenology", in terms of which one could compare the experiences that can be enjoyed by different animals.

The final chapter—**Educational Implications of Artificial Intelligence**—surveys some ways in which AI-research, and psychological work influenced by it, is relevant to the theory and practice of education. Insofar as theories within developmental psychology affect educational thinking, computational influences on such theories are of interest. Recent computationally informed work on "micro-development", for example, studies a child's growing mastery to a degree of detail that is not matched in more traditional approaches. Again, AI-based theory and computer technology (fundamentally different from behaviourism and Skinnerian teaching-machines) are beginning to provide educational tools enabling learners to explore an unfamiliar knowledge-domain in a relatively self-directed—and self-monitoring—way. A domain that will be increasingly important for the citizens of industrialized countries, and to some degree of the Third World too, is artificial intelligence itself: this chapter suggests ways of fostering the sort of "computer literacy" which will be needed by the general public as society makes increasing use of AI-technology. Also mentioned are early efforts to use LOGO-programming to help mentally and/or physically handicapped children to develop their intellectual potential (later results are reported in [Weir,1987]). Above all, this chapter argues that the view of "intelligence" implied by the computational approach recognizes knowledge and thinking to be essentially active, constructive, integrative, self-directed, and creative.

One hundred and fifty years ago Charles Babbage declared, "I was well aware that the mechanical generalizations I had organized contained within them much more than I had leisure to study, and some things which will probably remain unproductive to a far distant day" [*Ninth Bridgewater Treatise,* 1837]. The same could be said today by researchers at the forefront of computational psychology, for the abstract science of operations is still largely unexplored. New forms of computation (connectionist or otherwise), and new types of inference engine, will surely be discovered. These essays, I hope, will indicate why so many people now share Countess Lovelace's excitement at the prospect.

Chapter 2

Fashions of Mind

Only Princess Diana's wedding dress was awaited more impatiently, greeted more enthusiastically, and copied more slavishly than are new ideas in psychology. Because psychology lacks a generally accepted theoretical uniform that fits all figures and pleases all tastes, it is especially prone to changing fashions. Psychologists do not even agree about what basic items their science's wardrobe should contain - what the right questions are to ask. While some psychologists may be confident that they are posing the central questions, others will surely disagree. So from the unadorned statement that someone is a psychologist, one can infer very little about that person's professional beliefs, or even interests.

Given this disagreement over what style of theorizing best suits the mind, any new approach is likely to be hailed as the missing paradigm, the link transporting psychology from myth to science. The computational approach—in which minds are thought of as information-processing systems comparable in many ways to computers—is the most recent psychological fashion. But it is not the first intellectual style to be welcomed as psychology's saviour, nor is it the first to be mocked by those preferring different modes.

Distinct psychological fashions have been designed by such theorists as Sigmund Freud, Ivan Pavlov, Jean Piaget, B. F. Skinner, and R. D. Laing, but none of these has achieved the enduring status of a Chanel suit. Their popularity has waxed and waned over the years and varies among different groups. Workaday styles in psychology—such as intelligence tests and personality profiles—have been widely adopted for practical purposes, but many see them as disguising the true nature of what they are intended to display. And if we look to psychological accessories, whose designers are such fringe figures as Wilhelm Reich (of the Orgone Box), Werner Erhardt (of EST, or Erhardt Seminar Training), and Carl Janov (of the Primal Scream), it seems that no psychologist can be so maverick as to lack a body of faithful followers, while none is so authoritative as to persuade all comers of his or her theoretical infallibility. Psychology is not a unified church.

But, unified or not, it is a church. The different styles of psychology resemble religious sects, arousing emotional commitment and antagonism to a degree rarely seen in other branches of scientific inquiry. This is not surprising, for any denomination in the field—whether venerated as the science of mind, of brain, or of behaviour—has implications that bear on deep issues of self and society. So psychological theories typically arouse not only intellectual disagreement and rejection but also passionate denouncement and scathing ridicule.

As in more theological forms of sectarianism, psychologists will go to great lengths, or sink to surprising depths, in opposing those theoretical fashions they find unattractive. Even in the gentlemanly nineteenth century, the psychologist and philosopher William James remarked of the new, experimental statistical psychology that it "could hardly have arisen in a country whose natives could be *bored*. Such Germans as Weber, Fechner, and Wundt obviously cannot." By the 1920's the invective had intensified. J. B. Watson's brainchild, behaviourism, had conquered the American academies within a few years of its birth in 1913. E. C. Tolman sneeringly described it as "mere Muscle Twitchism", and William McDougall as "a most misshapen and beggarly dwarf"—a description that in the world of *haute couture*, would be damaging indeed. More recently, Noam Chomsky [1959] has ridiculed the preeminent behaviourist Skinner by saying that, according to Skinner's views on reinforcement, the best way to encourage an artist would be to stand in front of his paintings yelling "Beautiful!" at the top of one's voice.

But behaviourists are not the only theorists to be attacked. Freud himself has been accused of systematic intellectual dishonesty by the English philosopher Frank Cioffi [1970], and the German psychologist Hans Eysenck [1957] has viewed Freudian theory as a classic case of the Emperor's new clothes, mocking it with a suitably italicized account of a railway journey: the train is going very fast and *"we bob up and down in our seats;"* it *"enters a dark tunnel"*, the signal arms *"rise* as we approach *and fall* again as we pass"*, and we *"sharpen a pencil"* to write a postcard, but— horror of horrors—*"the point drops off."*

Borrowing the words of the seventeenth-century philosopher Thomas Hobbes, Guy Robinson [1972] has applied perhaps the most scathing dismissal—"When men write whole volumes of such stuff, are they not mad, or seek to make others so?"—to the most recent psychological fashion. This new mode is the computational approach, whose disciples describe the mind and thinking with concepts drawn from artificial intelligence and related forms of computer modelling. Artificial intelligence involves the use of computer programming to study the structure and function of knowledge. But unlike programs for calculating tax rebates or matching computer dates, which are rigid and inflexible, work in artificial intelligence focuses on *intelligent* information-processing abilities, which enable a system to cope flexibly with changing and largely unknown situations. The programs specify computations that enable computers to converse (by teletype) in natural language; to understand spoken speech; to recognize objects seen in widely varying positions or lighting conditions; to plan complex tasks involving unpredictable conditions; to make sensible guesses when specific knowledge is not available, and the like.

Computation in this sense does not mean mere counting, but *any* symbolic process of inference, comparison, or association. The symbolism may be numerical (for counting is one example of computation), or of some other form, such as verbal, visual, or logical. Seen from this viewpoint, the mind is a system for manipulating symbols. It contains many representations of aspects of the world (and other possible worlds), and a variety of rules for building, changing, comparing, and drawing infer-ences. Psychological questions, accordingly, concern the structure and content of mental representations and the ways in which they can be generated, augmented, and transformed. Thought, experience, and motivation—and the myriad differences among individual people that lead to the fascinating human pastime of gossip—are grounded in computational processes.

In the Middle Ages, for instance, the thoughts and actions of people who set off in search of unicorns, expecting to find them in the forest with their heads resting in the laps of virgins, were guided by a specific mental representation—the goal of finding a unicorn in those circumstances. We in the twentieth century can form similar representations; that is, we can think about mediaeval beliefs and ideas about unicorns. But we do not, as a consequence, guide our footsteps into the forest, because our minds represent the notion that unicorns do not exist. An essential precondition for purposeful, voluntary action—that the goal be believed, rightly or wrongly, to be at least *possibly* attainable—is thus not satisfied.

Suppose we were trying to suspend our disbelief in unicorns, or to discount it, and then to venture into the woods for a fanciful picnic, dressed appropriately in tunic and hose and carrying with us a silken halter. This would require a temporary transformation of our representation of unicorns so that their nonexistence was either not recognized, or else not allowed to veto the afternoon's plans. That is, the check on whether the plans were realistic would not be carried out, so that from the judgment "there are no unicorns" we would not draw the inference that "there is no point in forming the goal of finding a unicorn." Searching for unicorns, then—and also refusing or pretending to do so—are human activities that depend on the functioning of specific rules and representations in the mind. If these are transformed, by learning, reasoning, or fancy, then the person's thoughts and actions relating to unicorns will be different.

These differences in behaviour and experience may be subtle or coarse-grained, for the representations concerned are varied and complex. Planning a unicorn-hunt, whether for fun or for real, requires that our minds contain more than the concept of unicorns. We must also understand the concepts of virgin and of forest, and be able to represent their probable locations and recognize them when we get there. We must be able to plan how to reach the forest, and how to creep up on a virgin and a unicorn without frightening either. And if we hope to catch the unicorn, we must not forget the halter. If we cannot get one of silk, would a hempen one do instead? According to our current sensibilities, it probably would. But according to an older, magical, viewpoint, it might not.

The psychological interest here is not in which conception of unicorn-hunting is true and which is false, but how people can make such mental representations and be guided by them, regardless of whether they are realistic. Understanding how something is possible is more important, in this sense, than predicting what will actually happen. Of course, if someone believes a unicorn to be a sea-creature, half fish and half woman, we can predict that he will not search for unicorns in the forest. But the theoretical interest is in how the familiar concept of unicorn can be integrated with a person's powers of perception, planning, and persuasion, so as to generate a unicorn-hunt. This integration may be extremely complex, involving comparisons of priorities (what else might one do this afternoon?) and individual life-styles (which of one's friends would appreciate the enterprise?).

Even in the Middle Ages, though, life was not focused solely on unicorns. And today people solve problems of varying sorts— from cooking a meal to designing motorbikes to writing sonnets. Similarly, people hold beliefs of different sorts about different kinds of things, beliefs that are largely idiosyncratic and not always consistent with each other. As Walt Whitman said, "Do I contradict myself? Very well then, I contradict myself: I am large, I contain multitudes." An adequate theoretical psychology should help explain how all these problems and beliefs can coexist in an individual mind. It should address such fundamental questions as: How do people recognize different types of problems and classify some as tractable and others as hopelessly beyond our grasp? What mental processes enable us to build or to acquire our various beliefs? How do we interrelate them, by inferring one belief from another or by recognizing inconsistencies? If we decide not to tolerate an inconsistency, how do we transform our minds' content or organization, or both, accordingly? For example, how do we relate evolutionary biology and Christianity? Can they be mental bedfellows, and if so what sort of conceptual bolster might be needed to be put down the middle of the bed?

No one, at present, can answer all these questions. But they are the sorts of problems to which computational psychology is especially well suited, for they concern the ways in which we store, retrieve, compare, and transform various sorts of symbolically represented information. Indeed, psychological questions in general—whether they concern belief, problem-solving, purpose, choice, language, perception, memory, or even emotion—can be understood as computational questions about mental rules and representations.

A connoisseur of the history of psychological fashions might observe that the newly arrived computationalists are not the first to style the mind as a domain of symbolic representation and transformation. Freud, for example, thought of defense mechanisms as involving different sorts of psychological transformation. Introjection and displacement, for instance, transform the object of neurotic hatred in distinct ways: introjection shifts it from another person to oneself; displacement to some third person, conceived of as somehow analogous to—symbolic of—the original. Similarly, dreams and slips of the tongue involve strings of symbolic transformations, which depend on idiosyncratic associations and comparisons as well as on generally interpretable symbols (such as tunnels). But Freud's ideas in this regard, like those of other noncomputational psychologists, are suggestive rather than specific, vaguely expressed rather than rigorously defined. (His richly textured suggestions, intuitively plausible though they may be, are more akin to literature than to science.)

The computational approach, by contrast, offers precisely definable concepts, because a program has to be expressed clearly, as a set of instructions for specific symbol manipulations, if a computer is to accept it. The attempt to express vague concepts in computational terms can therefore help to clarify them (the previous example, Freudian defense mechanisms, is a case in point [see Colby, 1965; Boden, 1987, chs. 2-3]). If a program is written in some high-level programming language (one that more closely resembles human language than does the series of binary digits that the computer will ultimately act on), the programmer can ignore the more basic operations involved—much as we may think of a task in terms of some high-level goal, being unable to specify the details of how we tackle it. But, since clarity is essential, work in artificial intelligence provides a rich source of clear distinctions between many types of symbolic representation and interpretative process.

Moreover, this style of theorizing highlights process as well as structure, since a program has to tell the computer not only what to produce but also how to produce it. Non-computational psychologists often take psychological change for granted, assuming that it can be specified sufficiently by stating the initial and final mental states involved. However, the process of mental transformation is itself problematic. In programming, a failure to suggest a way in which a change might be effected will show up as a glaring gap over which the uninstructed computer cannot leap. Some computational account of how to make the leap must be supplied if the program is to function. In short, the pictures of the mind that are drawn in the computational style are more like movies than pinups.

Think, for example, what happens in our minds when we discern what someone means by the word *it* on any particular occasion. Consider this snatch of conversation from *Alice's Adventures In Wonderland* :

> "Even Stigand the patriotic Archbishop of Canterbury,
>   found it advisable - "
> "Found what?" asked the duck.
> "Found it", replied the mouse, rather crossly. "Of course
>   you know what 'it' means?"
> "I know what 'it' means when I try to find a thing", said

the duck. "It's generally a frog, or a worm. The question is, what did the Archbishop find?"

Obviously, in the duck's last remark "it" refers to the object found by the duck, whereas in the first sentence of the exchange "it" does not refer to an object at all (which is why the question here is *not* "what did the Archbishop find?"). Stating all the grammatical principles involved here (so as to say precisely what was the duck's mistake in asking *what* the Archbishop had found) is very difficult. And it is well-nigh impossible to suggest a series of psychological processes for interpreting the word *it* in its various uses (there have been three in this sentence so far!), processes that might explain what goes on in our minds when we understand everyday language. Or, rather, it is well-nigh impossible without the discipline of programming.

A common criticism of the computational approach to psychology is that while a computer program can achieve a certain result, such as recognizing a unicorn, playing chess, or interpreting the word *it*, people do not necessarily reach that result in the same way. While there are many different levels at which one might specify the way in which a program does something—it might do it in the same way as people under one description, but in a different way under another—one cannot pass directly from computation in a program to thinking in a person. Still, even psychologists who see the computational approach as radically misconceived often admit that it may be scientifically useful for generating hypotheses. Thus many who doubt that a computational methodology (still less, one based only on the computational concepts in use today) will answer all their questions are nonetheless prepared to use it, until its limits can be established.

The newly fashionable talk of computers and programs, however, is not acceptable in all salons, for many people see it as the "punk-gear" of psychology, as an aggressive rejection of traditional styles. From this viewpoint, the computational approach appears to offer a chilling picture of humanity that is not only false but also dangerously dehumanizing. It has been criticized as an obscene and deeply humiliating view, one that will deaden our personal responses and our valuation of purpose, desire, and emotional life [Weizenbaum, 1976]. It is bad enough, such critics complain, to say (with Freud) that we are driven by irrational drives and uncontrollable anxieties, or (with Skinner) that, like rats or pigeons, we are slaves responsive only to environmental conditioning. But to put people on a par with computers, they feel, is even worse than bringing us down to the level of unreasoning beasts. Little wonder, then, that such humanists accuse proponents of the computational approach of being "mad", or, worse, of seeking to make others so.

Like beauty, however, madness may be inthe eye of the beholder. These fears of the computational approach are mistaken. They rest on the failure to realize that describing something (whether person or computer) as a symbol-manipulating system is conceptually quite distinct from describing the physical hardware that embodies the computational powers concerned. The first description requires computational ideas, whereas the latter employs the terms of physics, chemistry, and physiology. Computational psychology does not support the mechanization of the world picture that has been brought about by the natural sciences, and by such "scientific" styles of psychology as behaviourism. Rather, it emphasizes the richness and subtlety of our mental powers, a richness that has often been intuitively glimpsed, at least by poets and novelists, but never theoretically recognized by psychologists. It admits the influence on our lives of shared cultural beliefs, of individual ideas, interests, purposes, and choice, and of self-reference and self-knowledge. And it provides rigorous hypotheses about the mental processes that underlie such influences and make them possible.

But, the power of fashion in psychology being so great, perhaps the computational style is a mere passing fancy? Is it a trendy fad born of a technological society, doomed to obsolescence because of its tin-can irrelevance to human realities? Or is it a classic, enduring contribution, the seed of the long-awaited general paradigm of psychology? Its being currently fashionable need not debar it from that role, for although fashion is largely ephemeral, some models last. While hats and halter-necks may be in or out, and colours change from season to season, shoes endure, despite changes in their details. How could they not, being so useful to soft-footed walking creatures?

The computational style in psychology will likewise survive, for it is so well suited to the representational anatomy of our minds. It offers a lasting insight into important mental features that other psychological approaches have recognized less clearly, or wholly ignored. It illuminates not only our cognitive or intellectual powers, but also our capacities for purposeful action and moral choice. It will change, to be sure, and some of its changes will doubtless be as shocking as next month's cover of *Vogue*. Many of the currently favoured types of computation will be superseded by others. Even today, different types are preferred by different theorists; some psychologists, for example, fashion computational theories for display on "connectionist" models—whose basic features are more brainlike than those of digital models are [Rumelhart & McClelland, 1986]. But the computational approach will endure, for it has provided a standard of rigour and clarity that must make us permanently dissatisfied with less.

Chapter 3
Is Computational Psychology Constructivist?

A "constructivist" psychology is most commonly thought of as one which employs some concept of *schema* or the like. "Constructivists" thus include not only Jean Piaget, but also F. C. Bartlett, J. S. Bruner, and R. L. Gregory. All these psychologists, despite their many differences, agree in emphasizing *top-down* influences in psychological processing. High-level structures or concepts, it is said, inform thought and perception through and through. Perception is then largely a matter of generating and testing—and if necessary adapting—hypotheses. And the background "theories" from which these hypotheses derive are the abstract schemata appropriate to the perceptual objects concerned.

Such a psychology, in addition, normally stresses the contribution of experience (learning or assimilation) to the content of schemata. Inborn influences may be allowed (as by Piaget, for example). But the theoretical emphasis is on the individual's own experience in the world. This is believed to be crucial even to such seemingly "basic" matters as the perception of three-dimensional (3D) shape.

Many computer models of psychological processes embody comparable top-down mechanisms. The scene-analysis approach in the early modelling of vision, for instance, relied on abstract schemata of cubes and other polyhedra to interpret the significant lines in the image. Often, these models even used schemata to help find the significant lines in the first place. The high-level knowledge that was stored in the schemata codified the likely 2D-appearance, or projection, of the 3D-cube (or whatever). Similarly, many language-using programs employ general concepts such as *script* to direct their processing top-down. And many parsing programs rely on high-level grammatical expectations in recognizing and looking for specific syntactic forms. A general rationale was offered for these approaches by Minsky's [1975] influential paper on *frames,* which argued for the ubiquity and necessity of top-down processing.

Not surprisingly, then, the computational approach is taken by many to depend on and to support constructivist psychology (I have argued this myself, in [Boden, 1982a]). However, this is to forget that there is really no such thing as "the" computational approach—unless by this we mean only some *very* general commitment to using computational ideas.

"Computational" psychologists, in the *broadest* sense of the term, all share three theoretical assumptions. They discuss the mind in terms of the properties of universal Turing machines, suggesting that every psychological phenomenon can be generated by some "effective procedure". They conceive of the mind as a representational system, and see psychology as the study of the various computational processes whereby mental representations are generated, organized, and transformed. And they think about neuroscience in a broadly computational way, asking what sorts of logical operations might be embodied in neural cells or networks.

These three characteristics define a general mode of psychological theorizing whose specific instances differ significantly. In particular, they are *not* necessarily "constructivist" in the (schema-driven) sense defined above.

Some computational models of perception, for instance, eschew schemata and top-down influences (and at first sight may seem almost "Gibsonian" in nature). D. C. Marr's [1982] work on low-level vision is a prime example. It is of interest here not only because of the challenge it appears to offer to constructivist psychologies, but also because of the quasi-Kantian character of Marr's approach.

Marr criticized the scene-analysis tradition for its inability to explain how we can see the 3D-shapes of arbitrary objects which we have *not* seen before. He regarded its constructivist stress on pre-stored schemata as a weakness, rather than a strength. In addition, he criticized its neglect of most of the information present in the visual (retinal) image. Those scene-analysis programs which could start from a grey-scale input (as opposed to a mere line-drawing) used line-finders at the earliest opportunity to convert it into the equivalent of a line-drawing. This highly impoverished representation was then used as the basis of all further (schema-driven) computation.

By contrast, Marr (like J. J. Gibson [1979]) insisted that the visual image itself is an extremely rich source of information. It should be exploited, not thrown away in the initial stages of visual processing. The image-information is so rich that it enables us to perceive the shape, texture, orientation, and position of unfamiliar objects for which we have *no* pre-established schemata. The theoretical problem for the psychologist, then, is to work out some principled way of reliably interpreting the information in the image—using bottom-up, rather than top-down, processes.

This type of visual interpretation must needs take account of the detailed physics of image-formation (Marr relied heavily on Berthold Horn's work in psychophysical optics). For only if we understand just how—according to the laws of optics—a given image could have been produced in the first place, can we hope to interpret it sensibly.

Physics is not enough, however. The reason is that, as far as physics alone is concerned, a given 2D-image could conceivably be generated by indefinitely many 3D-scenes—and *vice versa*. This is what makes it possible for a person visiting the "Hall of Mirrors" in a funfair to be confronted with many different (2D) images of one and the same (3D) body. Only if we have a guarantee that we are not creatures living in some exotic funfair-world, can we have any confidence in our visual interpretations.

One might object that no such guarantee is needed, at least for those visual perceptions that are corroborated by touch. But this presupposes that we can arrive at some specific visual interpretation to be corroborated. In a funfair-world, we could not do this, since we would have no reason to arrive at one "visual

interpretation" rather than another. The question of corrobora-
tion by touch thus could not arise. Conceivably, we might be
furnished with a retinal apparatus that presented us with a
varying display of light and shade, produced by the continuously
changing optical properties of the external world (like distinct
mirrors in the funfair). But this 2D shadow-show could be of no
practical use to us. We would, in effect, be blind.

Marr therefore argued that vision is in general possible *only* if
the visual system can take for granted certain abstract assumptions about the nature of the physical world—or, what comes to
the same thing, the principles of interpretation to be applied to
images. That is, Marr set himself the "Kantian" task of specifying
universal constraints, or ontological features, by virtue of which
perception is made possible. As we shall see, these constraints set
limits on the nature of visual systems, and also on the nature of
visible worlds.

The Kantian aspect of Marr's approach is reflected in his novel
definition of "computational psychology"—which he equated
with scientific psychology *tout court*. Marr argued that psychology should comprise explanations at three levels, of which the
first (which he called the "computational" level, despite the fact
that it is *not* concerned with *process*) is theoretically basic. This
level identifies the information-processing task which defines a
given psychological ability, and specifies the *universal* computational constraints that face any creature aiming to carry it out. In
general, the task will consist in effecting a mapping from one kind
of information to another, where the latter kind is more appropriate to the interests of the species. The computational theory
provides an abstract proof that a particular mapping is in principle possible.

The second—"algorithmic"—level takes account of the computational constraints identified at the first level, in specifying
the psychological processes, or computations, by means of which
the task is actually performed. These processes are defined in
terms of a particular system of representation for the input and
output information, which should be *proved* to be reliable by
reference to the first-level constraints. Though any putative

representation and algorithm must be justified in these terms, the computational (first-level) analysis in principle allows for various alternatives. Part of the psychologist's job is to compare these as to their computational efficiency and empirical plausibility. For example, Marr developed two different algorithms for stereopsis, each of which was grounded in his first-level analysis. (He criticized previous accounts of stereopsis for "computing the wrong thing": the image-properties concerned were not in fact semantically adequate to represent 3D-structure, as a computational (first level analysis would have shown.

The third, or "hardware", level concerns the specific mechanisms in which the representational processes defined at the second level are embodied in a given organism. There are even more degrees of freedom here than at the second level. Martians may indeed have eyes and brains made of green slime—provided that the physico-chemical properties of the slime are capable of supporting the computational processes defined at the algorithmic level. These, in turn, must compute broadly the same (2D-to-3D) functions that are computed by human brains. In short, the biology of vision may be highly variable, but the basic functions computed by visual systems are not.

On this view of psychology, then, the psychologist must start from an identification of the information-processing task that defines the class of phenomena concerned. Identifying the task will typically give a clearer understanding of what the ability in question *is*, quite apart from how it functions. (Whether this definition can fruitfully be applied to other areas of psychology is controversial: Marr himself saw syntactic parsing as the only obvious candidate.)

With respect to vision, Marr argued that the basic task is the mapping of the incoming light (a 2D-array) onto reliable—though not necessarily infallible—descriptions of the position, orientation, and depth of surfaces in the 3D-world.

But unless we have some notion of what the 3D-world can be expected to be like, there is no way in which we can be confident that a particular method of mapping is indeed reliable. This is where "quasi-Kantian" constraints come in. Marr saw the identification of these constraints as the basic scientific problem facing the psychologist, because only they can validate visual interpretation.

Four examples of such constraints that were suggested by Marr [1982, pp. 45-49, 113] are the *hierarchical, similarity, continuity,* and *smoothness* constraints:

> *The Hierarchical Organization Constraint* : The spatial organization of a surface's reflectance function is often generated by a number of different processes, each operating at a different scale.

> *The Similarity Constraint* : The items generated on a given surface by a reflectance-generating process acting at a given scale tend to be more similar to one another in their size, local contrast, colour, and spatial organization than to other items on that surface.

> *The Continuity Constraint* : In addition to their intrinsic similarity [guaranteed by the *similarity* constraint], markings generated on a surface by a single process are often spatially organized—they are arranged in curves or lines and possibly create more complex patterns.

> *The Smoothness Constraint* : Matter is cohesive, it is separated into objects, and the surfaces of objects are generally *smooth* in the sense that the surface variation due to roughness cracks, or other sharp differences that can be attributed to changes in distance from the viewer, are small compared with the overall distance from the viewer.

These constraints are used to justify the various methods of perceptual interpretation specified by Marr's visual algorithms. For example, his image-matching procedures for stereopsis give reliable information about depth only on the assumption that stereoptical disparity will vary *smoothly* almost everywhere. This assumption itself is based on the prior assumption that the physical distance from the observer to the visible surface of the object varies *continuously* except at object boundaries.

Since the role of the basic computational constraints is to ground (and simplify) visual processing so as to make vision possible, they have implications for the ontology of visible worlds. Any visible world, whether the viewer is a man or Martian, must have certain physical characteristics.

For example, the continuity constraint implies that most surfaces in a cognitively friendly world do not have random reflectance functions: they are patterned rather than chaotic. One may therefore expect to find striped, spotted, or dappled animals (for instance), whose markings form smooth contours on a surface. Hierarchical organization implies that a visible world will exhibit the "herringbone-tweed" phenomenon, in which (for instance) stripes on a surface consists of smaller stripes *on the same surface*. And the smoothness constraint means that a cognitively friendly world does not consist merely of sliced cakes or mosaic pavements, where the surfaces of neighbouring objects are all equally distant from the viewer.

Arguments at the abstract computational level are thus reminiscent of a Kantian transcendental deduction. They make universal claims about what the world must be like, and what see-ers must be like, if vision is to be possible. Visual systems have evolved (and should be engineered) so as to exploit specific computational constraints. And all seeing creatures must have a built-in epistemological bias toward the perception of worlds having the requisite general properties (hence the lesser emphasis on individual *learning*).

Kant's transcendentalism, of course, allowed that non-human creatures might have empirical schemata and categories very different from ours. Even the laws of physics might be different, for these too—according to Kant—are ultimately a feature of the human mind. For example, there might be some empirical world (that is: some community of rational creatures sharing the relevant epistemological biases) in which light follows curved paths, or in which reflectance-functions vary from moment to moment in accordance with some (to our minds, arbitrary) complex pattern. But Marr was not so Kantian as Kant. He would agree that some creatures might have perceptual capacities very unlike ours. However, he did not allow for a universe in which the laws of physics could be different. Consequently, any creature capable of using light to effect a 2D-to-3D mapping must live in a world with the requisite ontology—which is to say, a *visible* world, physically constrained in the same way as ours is.

Transcendental deductions are not immune to criticism, but they cannot be challenged experimentally. They are based on *a priori* argument, not on isolated facts gained through particular experience. Admittedly, Marr's "transcendental deduction" is not absolutely *a priori*, since it takes for granted empirical knowledge of the world, as opposed to world-independent metaphysics. It could therefore be challenged empirically, if one were to accuse Marr of misdescribing the general nature of the empirical world or (what comes to the same thing in this context) our knowledge of it. Indeed, an example of such a challenge is given below. But Marr's transcendental deduction is not based on, and cannot be contradicted by, the specific empirical knowledge gained by experimentation. It seeks to make psychology an axiomatic science whose axioms involve knowledge only of a highly general nature. Disputes at the computational level are therefore *a priori* in the sense that they concern issues which apply to all seeing creatures, not just to men—or Martians.

One such dispute centres on Marr's *smoothness* constraint. This has been criticized as over-restrictive, as not generally appropriate to the nature of the empirical world. It is true by and large that surfaces are smooth (neighbouring points being equidistant from the viewer), so that ocular disparity varies smoothly almost everywhere in the images of the two eyes. But in a significant number of cases they are not, yet depth-vision is still possible. An alternative, more general, constraint has been suggested which enables the stereoptic perception of depth in a wider class of cases (a larger set of possible worlds). This *ordering* constraint [Mayhew, 1983] is based on the fact that stereo-projection normally preserves the ordering and adjacency relationships of intensity-gradients in the two images—a "fact" that is deduced from the laws of optics, not inferred from experiments.

As in this example, the perceptual algorithms defined by Marr are primarily *bottom-up* in character. They are based on the physical properties of the image (such as ocular disparity and light-intensity gradients), rather than on hypotheses justified by pre-existing high-level schemata. Moreover, they are grounded in *local*, rather than *global*, computations. They use evidence each "packet" of which is drawn from a tiny part of the image, or of the particular representational level concerned (so are well-suited to a parallel architecture).

These two features distinguish them from the interpretative procedures favoured by constructivism as defined above (with reference to *schema-driven* processing). Indeed, in his early writings Marr devoted a good deal of energy to criticizing the top-down, holistic, approach of scene-analysis, and of constructivist psychologies in general. He saw his own theory of vision as a rival to schema-driven accounts.

It would be misleading, however, to suggest that Marr's psychology is non-constructivist through and through. For constructivism stresses *activity* on the part of the psychological subject. To construct is to *do* something (more specifically, to *build* something), as opposed to passively accepting what is given. Constructivism is thus fundamentally at odds with the classical empiricist tradition, which stresses the *data* input to the mind and neglects what the mind does with the data. This is why Kant's view is deemed constructivist, even though he did not appeal to perceptual schemata of distinct classes of object. Rather, he posited highly abstract principles and categories, such as *space, time, cause, identity, substance,* which he claimed organize the building of all our empirical knowledge. We have already seen that Marr's theory of perception is significantly similar to Kant's, which in itself suggests that he could be deemed a constructivist too.

To put this point in another way: According to today's constructivist psychologies, the things that are built in the mind are schemata, concepts, interpretations, models—in a word, *representations*. But representations are precisely what Marr's theory is about. (In this sense, he is *unlike* Gibson.) On Marr's view, perception is *by no means* direct, nor is it a passive acceptance or registration of input data. To the contrary, it is the end-product of a hierarchical series of representational processes, each of which constructs (*sic*) higher-level descriptions of the information computed at the lower level.

Neither a *representation* nor a *description* is something which exists "in the world": each is something that must be constructed by a mind. Marr defined a representation as a systematic set of descriptions, systematically derived, and his definition makes it clear that he has a constructive activity in mind: "A representation is a formal system for making explicit certain entities or types of information, together with a specification of how the system does this. A given representation thus generates a specific class of descriptions of the entities represented, some information being made explicit while other information is not. (The latter may be irretrievably lost, or it may be implicit—in which case it is in principle possible for it to be made explicit later. For instance, Marr's multi-level representation allows for the orientation of an edge to be made explicit *after* its length and position have been described.)

The distinction between different "levels" of representation rests in the different sorts of symbolic description that are constructed, or computed. In Marr's theory of vision, several levels are distinguished. These are hierarchically related, the primitives of one being defined in terms of the descriptions generated at the level below. For example, continuous *intensity-gradients* are used as evidence for *lines,* groups of which are described as *blobs,* and so on. In general, each successive representational level computes descriptions of a more abstract, or high-level, kind.

Insofar as it stresses the construction of representations, then, Marr's computational theory of vision is "constructivist" in a significant sense. But what of the schema-driven sense of "constructivism," with which we opened this paper?

Even with respect to this stronger sense of the term, Marr is not an unqualified anti-constructivist. Despite his early attacks on schema-driven models of vision, he himself came to accept that high-level schemata play an important role. Indeed, he tried to formulate principled ways in which whole classes of such schemata might be generated and compared.

For example, he adapted the notion of "generalized cylinder" to the description of the body-shapes of various animals. The main axes of the bodies of a man and a horse, for instance, are typically vertical and horizontal respectively. Moving to the next level of detail, one can identify minor axes representing the limbs. These, too, have a characteristically different disposition in man and horse. An image of a giraffe has a component axis whose connections with other body-axes enable it to be interpreted as representing a neck, and whose relative length and orientation distinguish it from a horse's neck—thereby distinguishing the animal-as-a-whole from a horse.

Whether "generalized cylinders" are adequate to ground representations of all 3D-shapes is another question. It is even problematic whether they could be efficiently adapted to the recognition of a horse lying down, or of a cat sitting by the fire. And what of the many other familiar shapes (whether natural or artificial) we encounter every day?

Further, even if something like Marr's bottom-up account is needed to explain what goes on when we see a 3D-shape for the first time, it does not follow that it is appropriate to the perception of more familiar objects. Perhaps systematic top-down hypothesis-testing is not always plausible in these cases, either. Many would argue that learnt perceptual "demons", which can be modelled for example by logically independent production-rules, are necessary for speedy perception. On this view, a familiar object might be recognized by the triggering of one such rule, there being no necessity for a series of computations comparing the image with a schema of the object-as-a-whole.

However, our original question did not concern the *truth* of schema-driven constructivism. It asked whether computational psychologies are, in general, constructivist.

We have noted the historical reasons why they are commonly taken to be so, and we have seen why this judgment cannot be generalized to *all* computational psychologies. Marr's work is just one example of a computational psychology that is *not* based on top-down, schema-driven, processing of the image as a whole. But even his theory can be described as "constructivist" in a broader, and significant, sense. Indeed, *any* computational psychology must be constructionist in this sense for *computations* are processes defined over representations. And representations, as Kant reminded us long ago, are constructed by living minds.

Chapter 4

Does Artificial Intelligence Need Artificial Brains?

Do you need a brain to be brainy? If by a "brain" we merely mean some physical organ that enables its possessor to do things intelligently, then of course you need a brain to be brainy. Even if "you" are a computer, the same applies. In this sense, artificial intelligence can't possibly do without artificial brains.

But what if by a "brain" we mean an organ of intelligence *that resembles the human brain* : what then? Perhaps some non-human intelligences could be brainy without one? If so, we might be able to build artificial intelligences without having to give them brains.

Let's try to get clear, first, about what sort of "resemblances" we have in mind here. We are *not* talking about whether or not something is made of protoplasm, nor about whether it has certain chemicals present in it. I assume that there is nothing magical about neurones: they are a part of the natural world. That is, they can in principle be described by physics and chemistry, just as bone and steel—and silicon chips—can too.

I assume, also, that there is no *special* physical property that is essential to intelligence, which is possessed only by brain-proteins. This second assumption might conceivably be mistaken—but neuroscience gives us no reason whatever to suspect that it is. Quite the contrary: the more brain scientists discover about this remarkable organ, the more they see it as a subtly complex physico-chemical system.

What this all comes to, then, is that the properties of the human brain that are relevant to its function as an organ of intelligence almost certainly have nothing to do *with what it is made of.* Rather, they concern *how it is organized* and *what it does.*

But this is precisely what leads many people to scepticism about artificial intelligence. For most work in artificial intelligence has been done, and still is being done, on machines whose fundamental organization differs from the brain in three important ways.

First, most computers are *digital* systems, in which the basic units either "fire" or they don't. The brain, on the other hand, is to a large extent an *analogue* device: synaptic activity varies continuously (and nerve-cells often fire "spontaneously" as a result). Second, digital computers are designed as *serial* devices, in which only one instruction is executed at a time. By contrast, the brain is a *parallel-processing* device: neurones have rich interconnections, which enable cells to encourage or inhibit their neighbours' activity. And third, digital computers are *general-purpose* machines, which can be used for indefinitely many problems. The reason is that they work by manipulating intrinsically meaningless formal symbols, whose meaning is ascribed by the human programmer and/or user. But many brain-cells are *dedicated* to one purpose. The visual cortex, for instance, contains cells that respond only to lines slanting in a particular direction, and the auditory cortex too contains highly specialized neurones.

Our original question can now be restated: Can only an analogue, parallel-processing, dedicated device be intelligent? Does any system that can do the same things as the human mind can do have to have an organ which is like a human brain in these ways? Or can artificial intelligence workers ignore human psychology and physiology? Can they simply get on with the job of building some artificial thinking-organ—which might be very different from the brain?

These questions are highly controversial. In the history of artificial intelligence (if something still so young can be said to have a history), the pendulum has swung from one answer to the other—and back again. In the early days, much research attempted to mimic the parallel functioning of the human brain. Then this research fell out of favour, and a quite different approach was preferred. Recently, however—and surprisingly—

some of the special features of the human brain are being taken seriously again.

You may feel that this swing-back of the pendulum is not "surprising" at all: *we* need brains to be brainy, so it's reasonable to expect that computers do too. But this is to ignore the reasons for the recent return to brain-like computer models.

For what do we mean by "brainy"—or by "intelligent"? Those whom we call "brainy" excel at abstract thought, such as mathematics, science, medicine, or even tax-law. And people regarded as "intelligent" are usually good at practical or verbal problem-solving, whether or not they are also "brainy" in the more academic sense. Occasionally, a person's brainpower is admired primarily because of an exceptional factual memory, like that needed to compete in *Mastermind*. In all these cases, people are marked out as intelligent because they can do things which most of us cannot.

By the same token, it is simply *irrelevant* to our everyday judgements of intelligence that someone can see things in the world around them, or speak their native language. These mental capacities receive no admiration, since almost all of us can see and speak so well—and so unthinkingly. Even common sense is not included in the meaning of "brainy" (so we can say without contradiction: "lots of brains, but no common sense"). Vision, language, and common sense are remarked upon only in their absence. When present, they are taken for granted. And, being thus taken for granted, they are commonly assumed to be relatively simple.

What is surprising about the history of artificial intelligence is that these everyday capacities have turned out to be much more difficult to automate than many of the achievements of our intellectual superiors. Traditional computers—which are *unlike* the brain—can do pretty well those things which we do badly. But they do very badly what we all do very well.

Give a (suitably programmed) general-purpose digital computer a problem in logic, maths, chemistry, or even medical diagnosis, and it may be able to solve it. Sometimes, it will do better than all but the best world-experts. Occasionally, it will surpass even them.

But ask it to see a face across a crowded room (as the song has it), and it will fail abysmally. Ordinary speech and commonsense reasoning, likewise, will be beyond it.

Some would say that this is merely because we haven't yet discovered how to write the "suitable" programs required. And certainly, if *any* computer could do these things, then—in principle—*some* serial-processing machine could do them too. But what is true in principle may be of little practical interest—not least because of the vast length of time that would be needed to do what is possible in principle. In practice, then, a different approach may be required to automate everyday human capacities.

We already know that evolution has come up with a different approach. The crucial organs of those living machines that can talk, think, and see—namely, human brains—are organized in a fundamentally different way. This is why some workers in artificial intelligence, namely those who wish to design computers to do those things which we all do so well, are increasingly looking, again, to the brain.

In the process, they expect to cast light on *just how* we ourselves do these things. For the computational processes in brain-like computers may be significantly similar to the processes going on in human brains. If so, the intellectual traffic will not be all one-way: neuroscience and psychology could benefit from artificial intelligence, as well as *vice versa*.

Consider computer vision, for instance. How could one enable a computer to see?

To avoid difficulties about consciousness (which only obscure the main point being discussed), let's agree that by "seeing", here, we'll mean the ability to reliably *describe* things in the external world, given information provided by a visual array, or image. And let's ignore aesthetic appreciation: never mind beauty, what about truth? That is, we'll take *seeing* to be the ability to use input light so as to produce *accurate descriptions* of things in the external world.

This descriptive ability would be an essential criterion of vision even if *conscious experience* were to be included also. The descriptions may be expressed in English or French, but they need not be: rats and squirrels show by their appropriate physical behaviour that in some interesting sense they can see. Further, the phenomenon of "blindsight" suggests that my exclusion of consciousness from our discussion is not wholly perverse. Someone with blindsight lacks *experience* of one half of their visual field, and cannot *describe verbally* an object lying in it: but they may nonetheless be able to put their hand in precisely the right position (and with fingers appropriately curved) to pick it up. (Perhaps some animals have visual systems enabling them to do this sort of thing, and no more.)

Our question, then, is this: How could a computer reliably report "That's a teddy-bear," or "I don't know just *what* that thing is—but it's about a foot long, with an undulating spotted surface slanting away from the ground. And it's a couple of yards away from me (a few inches in front of the large round object)"?

The earliest work in computer vision reflected the ideas about the brain that were current at the time [Boden, 1988, ch. 2]. People tried to build parallel-processing devices, analogous to neural networks, that would be capable of recognizing distinct visual patterns. (The fact that these "parallel-processors" were actually simulated on serial machines is irrelevant: as we shall see, their prime weakness lay in what they did, not in the machinery with which they did it.)

One such program was called *Pandemonium* [Selfridge, 1959], because its author described its action in terms of the simultaneous shouting of several information-processing units, or "demons". The demons were observant, but very narrow-minded. Each demon knew about, and watched out for, only one thing: perhaps a horizontal bar in the middle of the visual field, or a convex curve in the top right-hand corner. When a demon saw what it was looking for, it sent a message to the central master-demon. Each demon varied the loudness of its voice according to its judgment about the probability and the importance of its message. But each made its decisions independently: no demon could influence the loudness of its neighbours' shouting.

On the basis of the messages coming in from the various demons, the master-demon would decide what overall pattern was present. For example, the letter "F" would be reported by the master if it was told that there was a "mid-vertical", an "upper-horizontal", and a "mid-horizontal" shout. Suppose that, in fact, the vertical stroke was not *precisely* vertical: then the relevant low-level demon would whisper, rather than shout. But since no letter consists of only two horizontal bars, and since the precise tilt of the upright bar is irrelevant, the master would decide on an "F" in this situation too.

Later versions of *Pandemonium* allowed for several levels of demons. The lowest-level demon might look for tiny segments of black in the image (for instance, a tiny horizontal line). The next level would consist of demons seeking out entire letter-strokes (several contiguous horizontal-snippets could be accepted as a horizontal stroke). Next would be a level of "letter-demons", each of which would look for a specific letter (the E-demon would demand one more horizontal stroke than the F-demon would). There might even be "word-demons," looking for specific words (such as "OAT", "FAT", and "EAT"—of which each pair differs by one letter, and the last pair are distinguished by a single letter-stroke).

There is a clear analogy between these single-minded demons and the remarkable "feature-detector" cells in the visual cortex—which respond (for instance) only to a line of a certain orientation, or an edge moving in a particular direction. Indeed, it was the computational arguments about perception put forward by *Pandemonium's* programmer which first suggested that feature-detectors might exist. This was what prompted neurophysiologists to search for them (first in the frog's retina, later in the mammalian brain).

This is just one example showing that computational models of psychological processes may help neuroscience. Computer scientists can tell neuroscientists nothing about the *material* nature of the brain. But they may (as in this case) be able to suggest what sort of *functional* unit neuroscientists might fruitfully look for. Both approaches are necessary: the neural matter is of interest to us primarily because the psychological functions it supports.

It was precisely because of the computational *functions* necessary for sight had not been properly identified, that these early parallel-processing models of vision had to be abandoned.

Despite their apparently brain-like organization, systems such as *Pandemonium* were radically incapable of seeing (describing) solid objects—like cubes, pyramids, or teddy-bears. They were fairly successful at recognizing simple patterns (such as letters or doodles)—*provided* that these were of a certain size, presented alone, oriented the right way up, and centred in the visual field. But they could not *interpret* patterns *as* two-dimensional representations of three-dimensional objects.

The reason is that they knew nothing about the third dimension, nor about how three dimensions can be projected into two. They responded to patterns as mere *patterns*. This suffices for the recognition of alphanumeric characters: there is no need to move into the third dimension to recognize "A" or "B". But for ordinary vision, it does not.

What seeing creatures need to see are things in the real world—food, predators, and pathways. Admittedly, mere patterns are sometimes biologically important. For instance, the red spot on a chick's bill may be the trigger that leads the mother-bird to feed it; and superficial patterns on fur or feathers are often crucial in releasing courtship behaviour. In general, however, vision is not *pattern-recognition,* but *image-interpretation.*

It follows that the mere counting of pattern-properties cannot suffice to enable a system to see. As this point was realized, the pendulum in computer vision swung away from computerized neural nets. Research turned instead to visual *interpretations,* images being viewed (*sic*) not as patterns but as representations of the real world [Boden, 1987, chs. 8 & 9].

These interpretations were justified by projective geometry, which tells us how solid objects of certain types would appear to an observer from different points of view. So systematic geometrical knowledge about 2D-to-3D mapping was built into computer-programs for "scene analysis" (as opposed to "pattern recognition"). These programs used their stored knowledge to build sensible 3D-descriptions of objects, given depictions of those objects in 2D-line-drawings. A drawing of a cube, for instance, would be recognized *as* a representation *of a cube.*

In general, a scene-analysis program could interpret line-drawings of those types of object which it knew about already. High-level knowledge about a given class of objects would be used to guide the visual interpretation: thus these programs "knew what to look for" in the 2D-image.

For example, they knew that the corner of a cube may appear in an image as a fork-shaped vertex, an arrow-shaped vertex, or an ell-shaped vertex. Given optimal lighting conditions, so that no edges are obscured, projective geometry guarantees that it simply *cannot* appear in any other way. What is more, an arrow-shaped vertex in the image *can only* correspond to, or represent, a convex real-world corner: one that points towards the eye. (See for yourself: try watching one corner of cube, gradually turning the cube towards and away from you.)

Since they knew what to look for, these programs could adapt to poor lighting-conditions, to some degree. Thus if two adjacent cube-corners had been found (depicted by two linked vertices in the image), they might deliberately look in the appropriate parts of the image for lines fainter than would normally be acceptable. This was possible partly because of the *serial* processing: interpretations of image-parts that had already been achieved could be used to influence the interpretation of image-parts looked at later.

It's no accident that my main example here has been a cube, rather than the teddy-bear mentioned earlier. Teddy-bears were, in effect, invisible to scene-analysis computers. Such cuddly toys could not even be identified by these programs as *solid objects.* And no teddy-bear could be described by them as something (albeit an un-nameable something) with a smooth furry surface, having bits sticking out here and there, and two shiny, round bumps near one end.

There were three basic reasons for the invisibility of teddy-bears. First, because of the simple projective geometry used by scene-analysis programs, only objects with straight edges (or extremely simple curves) could be described by them. Second, these systems had to be pre-programmed with detailed knowledge of what they were going to see, if they were to see at all. Since they were not told (and moreover could not be told) what teddy-bears look like, they had no way of finding their salient curves or surfaces—no way of seeing them.

And third, scene-analysis programs could not see localized depth or surface texture. Even a fabric-covered *cube*, such as one might give to a very young baby) could not be described by a scene-analysis program as furry or smooth. And no glass cube could be seen by them as shiny.

The human brain is not so limited. It can interpret images of very unfamiliar objects, inferring a great deal of 3D-information about them in the process. If you have never seen a teddy-bear before, you won't be able to recognize or name one. But you will be able to *describe* it in detail, as a specific (unfamiliar) physical object. That is, you can see its shape, surface-texture, orientation, size, position, and colour; and you can distinguish certain parts of it, such as its shiny glass eyes sticking out from the main surface.

Computer-vision programs, if they are to be useful to us in a wide range of circumstances, ought to be able to do the same sort of thing.

Some recent computer-systems *can* do so (at least to a significant degree) [Mayhew & Frisby, 1984]. What's more, they are decidedly "brainlike" in certain ways. Once again, the emphasis is on parallel processing, and multiple interactions within networks of elementary dedicated units. But these latest systems are significantly different from *Pandemonium*.

Their difference is theoretical rather than mechanical: their superiority owes less to modern technology as such (even now, most "parallel-processors" are actually simulated on traditional digital machines) than to our deeper understanding of *what it is,* and *how it is possible,* to see something as a solid (3D) object, given only a 2D-image. (Scene-analysis workers took such questions seriously, but as we have seen they did so in an insufficiently general way.)

The theory implicit in the new "brainlike" machines is the physics of image-formation. For the function and interconnections of the individual processing units are carefully engineered (and/or programmed) according to detailed optical knowledge. The optics concerned does not merely describe the behaviour of light, considered in itself. Rather, it deals systematically with the ways in which light can be reflected from *physical surfaces* of various sorts.

Nor is theoretical optics limited (as scene-analysis was) to telling us what images could represent the corners of cubes, or the tips of pyramids. It answers much more general questions, such as: how is light reflected from a particular sort of surface?; or from a surface (or tiny part of a surface) which happens to be oriented at a particular angle relative to the viewer?; or from a surface at such-and-such a distance from the eye (or differing distances from the two eyes)?

In these "connectionist" machines, each processing unit is dedicated to seeking a specific type of perceptual (3D) interpretation for the (2D) image-part it looks at. The image corresponding to the overall surface of any physical object is made up of many tiny areas, or point-images. Neighbouring point-images are likely to be similar, because neighbouring surface-points are usually similar. For example, a furry point is usually surrounded by other furry points, and a glassy point by other glassy points: only round the edge of a glass-eye, for instance, will this not be true. Difference-boundaries in the image such as this one may therefore be interpreted as real boundaries between distinct objects in the real world.

But of course, in a world where tigers and dalmatians exist, we would not want *every* discernable difference-boundary in the image to be interpreted in this way. The white and black patches on a dalmatian's coat are not different objects: they are part of one and the same physical surface, attributable to one and the same thing (the dog). In general, local differences in the image may be *organized*, so as to reflect (*sic*) surface markings (such as spots and stripes), and surface contours (such as the gentle curves of a teddy-bear's face).

So, much as *Pandemonium* had several levels of "demons" (looking for stroke-fragments, letter-strokes, whole letters, and words), these recent visual systems have several levels of description available to interpret the image. Some units look for certain sorts of organization within the descriptions arrived at by lower-level units.

One of the ways in which image-points can be described by these new brainlike machines is in terms of their distance from the viewer. This is crucial in deciding where one object starts and another begins. For if a sudden depth-disparity is noticed at a series of neighbouring points in the image, these are taken to correspond to the edge of the physical object concerned (such as the side of the bear's eye, or leg). In consequence, these machines could pick out (as you could, too) a dalmatian dog lying on a black and white spotted rug. And they could do this even if they had never seen a dalmatian before. (They would not know it was a *dalmatian*, but that is a different matter.)

The interconnections between the individual units do not merely enable messages to be passed from lower-level to higher-level units (as in *Pandemonium*). They also allow for feedback between units. This feedback takes into account the *physical possibilities* of images in various real-world situations.

This would be helpful, for example, in distinguishing a black image-patch caused by a black spot on a dog's coat from an *immediately contiguous* black image-patch caused by markings on the rug the dog was lying on. Suppose that some early processing-units had described this part of the image as "one" black patch (for that is how it appears, in the image). If the depth-detecting units were then to decide that there was a line of depth-disparity running through this area, they could pass messages to the patch-detecting units concerned, so as to *inhibit* them from describing this as "one" patch (ascribable to "one" surface). Conversely, feedback *facilitating* certain units might occur. In effect, then, these newfangled demons not only shout more or less loudly on their own account, but tell each other to shout more or less loudly, so as to arrive at a *mutually consistent* set of shouts.

In short, we have here a parallel-processing system, whose units are analogue rather than digital (for they can shout more or less loudly), and which are dedicated to seeing certain things (the units which can see depth cannot see lines or blobs). That is, we have something significantly like a brain. And at least some of the 2D-to-3D computations done by these systems are arguably like those carried out by our own visual cortex. For instance, stereopsis (depth-vision that relies on disparities between the images presented to the two eyes) is much better understood as a result of this recent computer-modelling research.

But this does not mean that all work in computer-vision not based on brain-like machines is a waste of time. The need for detailed knowledge of optics was shown partly by previous work in the very different computational tradition of scene-analysis. And there are many problems about vision which remain. For example, maybe once you are familiar with dalmatians you *do not have to* build your dalmatian-interpretation "bottom-up", by using each individual mark on the dog's back. Admittedly, you may have to do something like this (perhaps even consciously) if you are shown a dalmatian lying on a black-and-white rug. But what you *can* do is not necessarily what you usually *do* do. The "top down" processing that enables you to use your high-level knowledge to see quickly and efficiently in everyday situations (no confusing rugs) may rely on methods more readily associated with traditional artificial intelligence.

In sum, maybe you don't need a brain to be "brainy". But there are strong reasons for believing that *any* competent visual system—whether engineered or evolved—must have a basic organization broadly similar to the human brain. This is necessary in order to achieve the computational functions necessary for the 2D-to-3D mapping which is essential to vision. But *functions* are where it's at: protoplasm has nothing, essentially, to do with it.

Chapter 5
Intentionality and Physical Systems

I

Intentionality is characteristic of many psychological phenomena. It is commonly held by philosophers that intentionality cannot be ascribed to purely physical systems. This view does not merely deny that psychological language can be reduced to physiological language. It also claims that the appropriateness of some psychological explanation *excludes* the possibility of any underlying physiological or causal account adequate to explain intentional behaviour.

This is a thesis which I do not accept. I shall argue that physical systems of a specific sort will show the characteristic features of intentionality. Psychological subjects *are,* under an alternative description, purely physical systems of a certain sort. The intentional description and the physical description are logically distinct, and are not intertranslateable. Nevertheless, the features of intentionality may be explained by a purely causal account, in the sense that they may be shown to be totally dependent upon physical processes.

II

The terms "intentional" and "intentionality" have been used in differing ways by different writers. Contemporary discussions of intentionality often draw heavily upon Brentano's account [Brentano, 1874]. Brentano used these terms primarily in speaking of objects of thought, or mental events, such as man's thought of a horse or a unicorn, or his belief that the earth is round or that it is flat. But in contemporary usage "intentionality" is commonly given a somewhat wider sense, such that *intentional* sentences or verbs are identified as sentences or verbs whose meaning involves the notion of the direction of the mind upon an object. Accordingly, intentional verbs include not only "believe", "wish", and "wonder", which have often been said to signify mental events—but also such items as "ridicule", "worship", and "hunt", which signify overt behaviour guided by thought [Kneale, 1968]. I shall be using the words in this sense, so that I shall regard as "intentional" all behaviour that is guided by thought, or which requires for its explanation the notion of the direction of the mind upon some object. Any behaviour that is guided by the purposes, desires, beliefs, concepts, or ideas of a psychological subject will therefore qualify as intentional behaviour.

Brentano believed that intentionality is peculiar to psychological phenomena alone, and that it thus provides a criterion by means of which the mental may be distinguished from the non-mental. According to Brentano, intentionality is both a necessary and a sufficient criterion of the psychological. I shall not discuss the view that *all* psychological phenomena (including bare sentience and pain) are intentional. Rather, I shall be concerned with the view that intentionality cannot be based in a purely physical system, that there is some sharp logical *and* ontological distinction between intentional and physical phenomena.

R. M. Chisholm [1967] has tried to express the difference between the mental and the physical in terms of purely logical distinctions. He hopes to find some list of logical properties which characterizes all and only intentional sentences, and which could therefore be used as a clear criterion of the psychological. One of his motives is that of supporting Brentano's thesis that no physical phenomena can be intentional. For Chisholm says that, if it can be shown that the sentences that we use in describing intentional psychological phenomena have logical properties which are not shared by sentences describing physical phenomena, then "the basic thesis of physicalism and the unity of science is false." I shall return to this claim shortly, but shall first say a little about Chisholm's suggested list of logical criteria.

Chisholm's original list was put forward in his book on *Perceiving* [1957], but it has been amended by him more recently [Sellars & Chisholm, 1958; Chisholm, 1963]. Four of the criteria he has suggested are: failure of existential generalization; nonextensional occurrence; no implication of embedded clause or its negation; and referential opacity.

It is clear that many intentional sentences *do* satisfy one of these four criteria. For instance, the first picks out the sentence "John is thinking about a horse," for from the truth of this sentence we cannot derive the truth of "There exists some horse which John is thinking about." By contrast, the nonintentional sentence "John is riding a horse" does imply the existence of some horse. Secondly, nonextentional occurrence picks out the sentence "Plato believed that Socrates was a philosopher;" for from it we cannot infer "Plato believed the world was round." It thus differs from a nonintentional sentence like "Either Socrates was a god or Socrates was a philosopher." Thirdly, from "Plato believed that Socrates was snub-nosed," we can infer neither that Socrates was, nor that he was not, snub-nosed. But from non-intentional sentences such as "It is true that Socrates was snub-nosed" or "Socrates' difficulties in breathing were due to the fact that he was snub-nosed," we can derive the truth of the embedded clause. Finally, the criterion of referential opacity picks out the sentence "Joe Martin believed that Dewey would be Truman's successor," for we cannot derive the sentence "Joe Martin believed that Dewey would be Eisenhower." By contrast, the sentence "Joe Martin had lunch with Truman's successor" *does* imply "Joe Martin had lunch with Eisenhower," simply because Truman's successor and Eisenhower were one and the same person.

However, these four criteria fail to characterize intentional sentences exclusively. For, while many intentional sentences satisfy one of them, so also do some clearly nonintentional sentences. For instance, failure of existential generalization applies to "The dam is high enough to prevent any future floods". Nonextensional occurrence covers "It is necessarily true that if

Socrates was a member of the class of philosophers, then Socrates was a philosopher." No implication of the embedded clause or its negation is involved in the sentences "It is contingent that Socrates was snub-nosed" and "Possibly what caused the power-cut was that the swan flew into the wires." And referential opacity characterizes "It is necessarily true that if Dewey was Truman's successor, then Dewey was Truman's successor" None of these sentences is intentional in the sense of including a verb whose meaning involves the direction of the mind upon some object; indeed, none of these sentences appears to be psychological in any sense.

[Logically intentional sentences such as those cited above, in fact, may be implicitly psychological. They all involve oblique contexts, depending explicitly or implicitly on the quotation of thoughts in *oratio obliqua*. For instance, sentences using modal qualifiers such as "necessary", "possible", and "impossible" do not directly assert or deny the sentential phrases within them, but obliquely assert something about them. In each case, what they assert is that if a psychological subject decides to pick one of these sentences as his object of thought, he should regard it in a particular way. Thus to say "Possibly, the power-cut was caused by a swan flying into the wires" is to say that our scientific knowledge about electricity justifies the assertion that such an event could have caused a powercut, and that our general knowledge about the district justifies the assertion that there may have been swans nearby, but that such specific evidence as we actually have does not imply that this succession of events did in fact occur. Even an example like "The dam is high enough to prevent any future floods"—which appears to be a statement about *a physical object* (the dam), not about any mind whatsoever—may be interpreted as meaning that the logical possibility that there might be floods is empirically excluded by contingent facts about the construction of the dam. So nobody need fear that there will be floods: a person—or, one might add, a computerized "expert system" for flood-control—who is informed of the height of the dam can infer that no flooding will take place. These suggested interpretations treat logically intentional (and *prima facie* nonpsychological) sentences as propositions about propositions, not as propositions about the world. And propositions are, roughly, thoughts attributable to thinkers. Accordingly, if this type of interpretation can be correctly applied in all cases of logical intentionality then the class of sentences denoted by the logical definition is identical with the class denoted by the psychological definition.]

Chisholm has suggested that nonextensional occurrence and referential opacity can be saved as criteria by a modal condition that specifically excludes noncontingent sentences such as those used in the examples above. And he has offered two further criteria that purport to identify intentional prefixes (such as "John believes . . ."), in terms of the logical properties of the sentences into which these prefixes are inserted, and of closely related sentences such as the universally or existentially quantified forms. But, as L. J. Cohen [1968] has shown, these criteria also fail to provide necessary and sufficient conditions for the psychological. To be sure, each criterion clearly characterizes many intentional sentences, and clearly does not characterize most nonintentional sentences. They may therefore be useful in comparing intentional with nonintentional phenomena, and I shall refer to them again later on. But, as a purely logical criterion of the psychological, Chisholm's list fails. Cohen [1968, p.142] has remarked that:

> The situation seems a characteristically philosophical one. Only by question-begging definitions of intensionality [sic] and/or psychologicalness shall we ever demonstrate, it seems, that the logical property of intensionality affords a sufficient and/or necessary condition of a proposition's constituting a psychological description.

That is, if we were to formulate necessary or sufficient logical conditions of intentionality, the universal coincidence of intentionality and the psychological would be merely trivially true.

I therefore shall not attempt to draw up a list of such conditions, but shall rely rather on the more familiar (though less clearly analyzed) notion that many psychological phenomena involve the direction of the mind upon an object. These are the phenomena which I shall classify as "intentional"

I quoted earlier Chisholm's claim that if intentional sentences are logically unique, then the basic thesis of physicalism and the unity of science is false. This claim is a very strong one. It does not merely deny that intentional statements can be translated into or replaced by nonintentional ones without loss of meaning. Nor is it merely the claim that, once having identified a (behavioural) phenomenon in intentional terms, we cannot properly go on in the same breath to explain it by laws expressed in nonpsychological categories. It is the claim that there can be no necessary and sufficient causal explanation of any behavioural phenomenon as described in nonpsychological terms, if that phenomenon can also be correctly described as "intentional". The unity of science is indeed threatened, since this view implies that no neurophysiological explanation of psychological phenomena is in principle possible: if the body is a purely mechanistic system, then our intentional behaviour cannot be completely determined by bodily causes.

Clearly, a type of example that would strongly support this view would be a case where a bodily event, even when initially described in nonpsychological language, required a psychological explanation. For if the behaviour had been initially identified and described as intentional, the necessity of an intentional explanation might be said to be due merely to a difference between causal (physical) and psychological *language*. From this it would not follow that there was any *ontological* distinction (threatening "the unity of science") such that the phenomenon could not properly be alternatively described in purely causal terms. To take an analogy: it would seem at least logically *odd*, and perhaps *improper*, to say: "That dog, Fido, is the father of that organization of carbon, nitrogen, phosphorus, and water;" but, nevertheless, a puppy could be appropriately so described in a different context. From the category-difference between "father" and "phosphorus" it does not follow that biology and chemistry cannot be parts of a unified science.

So, in rebutting Chisholm's view, I shall first discuss an example of behaviour that seems to require a psychological explanation *even* when it is initially described in the language of muscle-movements, and which has often been regarded as a relatively clear case of the mind controlling the body. I shall try to show how a physical or physiological explanation could, in principle, account for this case; and how such an explanation could underlie the intentional characteristics of behaviour.

III

My example is a type of pathological behaviour that is commonly regarded as clearly psychosomatic in origin. When the physician Charcot was in charge of the *Salpetriere* hospital in the late nineteenth century, his attention was drawn to certain strange cases of paralysis and anaesthesia—"strange" in three ways.

Firstly, there was no apparent physical injury or record of physical accident that could account for the paralysis or for the anaesthesia. Secondly, under hypnosis the "paralysed" limb would move, and the "anaesthetized" skin would be sensitive to stimuli that had no comparable effect before the hypnotic state was induced.

This certainly suggested that there was no *simple* bodily explanation in terms of an injured sensory or motor nerve (or group of nerves) supplying the region in question. Moreover, the methods used to hypnotize the patients were such as to encourage the opinion that the phenomena required psychological explanation, explanation in terms of the mind rather than the body. Charcot, and his associates and pupils (one of whom was the young Freud) did indeed explain these strange paralyses and anaesthesias in psychological terms, and so did many other workers who later discussed these cases. The precise theoretical terms they appealed to differed, as a few examples will show. The temporary paralysis of the limb was variously attributed to sexually based "hysteria" [Charcot, 1890]; to "suggestion" [Bernheim, 1886]; to a "secondary consciousness" [James, 1890]; to "dissociation of the personality" [Janet, 1906; Prince, 1906]; and even to the workings of a separate, and subordinate, personality partially free from control by the dominant personality or self [McDougall, 1926].

We may feel that such "explanations" in terms of "the mind", "suggestion", or "subordinate personalities" are merely evasive labels for the problem, pseudo-explanations that have no place in a rational science and which should be replaced by neurophysiological explanations of proven respectability. Moreover, while a *simple* bodily explanation of the type I have mentioned is obviously excluded, since the muscle-movements that never occur in the unhypnotized state *do* occur under hypnosis, we may feel able to suggest in general terms how such phenomena may be satisfactorily explained. For the higher centres of the nervous system may be assumed to be capable of controlling the peripheral nerves so as sometimes to put them temporarily out of action, perhaps by blocking their normal paths of communication with other nerves. Consequently, the brain may function as a switching mechanism, such that a given muscular movement is sometimes possible, and sometimes not. In this way, we may feel, all mention of the mind and all psychological terms can be avoided—and so much the better for that.

But then we shall be brought up against the third way in which these "hysterical" phenomena are *strange,* and this is not so easily dealt with. The third feature itself has two aspects. Firstly, it is found that the extent, or boundaries, of the paralysis or anaesthesia is often of such a nature that it cannot be explained by any purely anatomical account: that is, one referring to a specific nerve or nerves being put out of action, whether because of lasting injury or because of temporary inhibitory control by the higher centres of the brain. The embryo grows on a segmental plan, with one pair of sensory and motor nerves supplying each segment; as a result, each nerve in the adult is distributed over a specific and clearly demarcated area, whether a particular group of muscles or a particular patch of skin. In these strange cases of hysterical paralysis, the muscles affected may not correspond to any group of muscles supplied by one or more nerves; similarly, the anaesthetic area of the skin may have limits that do not coincide with any anatomical boundaries corresponding to nervous distribution.

So far, then, we have a puzzle. But the second aspect of this third feature of strangeness suggests to us a solution that may seem even more bizarre: the boundaries of the malfunction, whether paralysis or anaesthesia, may not correspond with real anatomical boundaries but they do correspond with something else—to wit, the layman's *idea* of anatomical boundaries.

For instance, in everyday life any arm is conceived of as a total unit that starts at the shoulder and extends down to the fingertips; its upper boundary is somewhat vague, but is roughly equivalent to the line of the arm-hole in a sleeveless shirt. Similarly, a hand is conceived of as a unit bounded roughly by a line around the wrist, and so on. And the anaesthesia, in the cases we are considering, extends over *all* and *only* the skin covering the hand, or the arm, *as so defined;* likewise, the paralysis covers all and only the movements of *what the patient thinks of as* his hand, or his arm. Anatomically, the nerves supplying these areas also supply other (unaffected) areas. But the patient, we may assume, is like most of us unaware of these anatomical niceties. He has probably never even noticed that when part of his hand "goes to sleep" after his leaning heavily on his elbow, the side of his ring-finger next to his little finger will have lost its feeling, as will the little finger also, but the other side of the ring-finger will not. To him, a finger is a finger, and unless such facts are pointed out to him he just does not think of it as in any way naturally divided down the middle.

It seems, then, that we have found an explanation for at least one strange aspect of the hysterical paralysis or anaesthesia: its precise boundaries on the skin. But this explanation refers to a specific aspect of the patient's mind, namely his concept of, or thoughts and beliefs about, his "arm" or his "hand" and so on. It seems that we are forced to mention those psychological phenomena in explaining the particular motor or sensory malfunction concerned, and it is not at all clear that we could reasonably hope to give a neurophysiological account without mentioning these beliefs, or concepts, of the patient. The strange hypothesis of a subordinate personality being responsible for the paralysis or anaesthesia at least looks more respectable now that we see that explanation must be in terms of beliefs; for beliefs can be attributed to persons and cannot be predicated of brains.

But how can this be? How *can* a person's concept of an arm affect his bodily reaction in such a manner? And does such psychosomatic control disprove the basis thesis of physicalism?

IV

Can we postulate any physiological mechanism corresponding to the concept of a person's mind which would result in the behaviour I have described? Or could we simulate a hysterical paralysis in some artificial physical system? And, if so, could a causal description of the physical mechanism make any intentional or functional explanations redundant? In this section I shall approach these questions in a general form; in the following section I shall develop an example in clarification.

The crucial step is for us to postulate that the brain somehow builds up *representations* or *models* reflecting various features of the environment; and that these models mediate between stimulus and response in determining the behaviour of the organism as a whole. Being partly determined by them, behaviour will naturally reflect their features.

It may be clear from the structure of behaviour that some representation of the world is available to the organism. For example, a passerine chick will crouch the first time it sees a hawk flying, and a female stickleback will respond in a species-characteristic fashion to her mate's "dance"; these responses require the discrimination of one particular stimulus-class from others, and so we postulate some (innate) mechanism which is sensitive to this stimulus-class and which thus functions as a "model" in the relevant sense. Similarly, in the pathological case I have described we are justified, on behavioural grounds, in saying that the patient has a certain representation, or "idea", of *a hand*. As we shall see, we may think of this "idea" either in psychological (functional) terms, or in physiological (physical) terms. In postulating cerebral models underlying behaviour we must initially identify them *via* behavioural features, but we may then enquire as to their neurophysiology.

A major source of the concept of cerebral models as controlling behaviour is K. J. W. Craik's [1943] discussion, in which he said:

> By a model we thus mean any physical or chemical system which has a similar relation-structure to that of the process it imitates. By "relation-structure" I do not mean some obscure nonphysical entity which attends the model, but the fact that it is a physical working model which works in the same way as the process it parallels in the aspects under consideration at any moment.

Craik discussed these models in very general terms, but his main point was that the brain may model environmental or abstract features that cannot properly be predicated of the models themselves. A cerebral model of a hand is not to be thought of as a little hand, but as something which *in certain respects* resembles a hand. As we shall see in the next section, a model of a hand might or might not be analyzable into independent models of parts of the hand (such as five fingers and a palm). And the relevant "relation-structure" might involve not only features such as colours and shapes, but also the linguistic system learnt by the subject. In many cases of human behaviour, the representation required to generate them may be nothing short of an internalized language.

It may be objected here that this notion of "modelling" is too wide to be useful, since language can express "certain respects" in which *any* object resembles *any* other. But the basic sensory discriminations that enable us to "fit" our language to the world must rely on some parallelism of physical relation-structures in the nervous system and the environment respectively; it is for the psychologist and the neurophysiologist to discover exactly which these parallels are. If any environmental property A is to be represented in the nervous system, there must be some neural property a that can have a range of values dependent on some different values of A. (A creature with no light-sensitive cells will not be able to see.) The range of possible values of a may parallel the range of A more or less closely. (A seeing creature may be colour-blind or not.) If different values of a are to be reflected in the behaviour of the organism as a whole, then they must differentially influence the (typically cerebral) nervous parameters controlling overall behaviour. (The retinae of cats and some fish are capable of colour-discrimination; but the animals themselves are colour-blind, since their central nervous systems are not of sufficient complexity to store this information picked up at the periphery, and so it is lost.) The values of a, b, and c must sometimes be directly determined by environmental features A, B, and C, if the organism is to acquire any information about the external world in its interactions with the environment. But the values of a, b, and c may also be determinable relatively indirectly, so that representations or models of (actual or hypothetical) environmental features may be generated independently of experience of those features. Given appropriate values of the relevant parameters we could say that an organism had a model of *a purple cat*, even though no such animal exists.

As yet we are not able to attribute any particular cerebral representation to any living organism merely by identifying specific values of certain neural parameters. For very little is known about the detailed nature of the parameters crucial to complex brain-function, or about the way in which cerebral models of the environment may be built up (but see [Lettvin, Maturana, Pitts, & McCullough, 1959; 1961; Young, 1964]). We can, to be sure, record the response of a single cortical cell which (earlier in the particular experimental session concerned) has been found to correlate with the presentation of a specific stimulus-class—for instance, *straight lines lying in a particular orientation* [Hubel & Wiesel, 1959; 1962] or *frequency of auditory tone rising* [Evans & Whitfield, 1964]. But we cannot give a neurophysiological identification or description of the cerebral cells characteristically active (or the neural parameters involved) when someone sees, thinks of, fears, or searches for *a purple cat*. We cannot specify the cerebral model of a *purple cat*, or that of *a hand*; we can only postulate such models on behavioural grounds, and hypothesize that they correspond to actual neurophysiological mechanisms. [Insertion: Since this paper was written, single-cell neurophysiological recordings have identified cells in the monkey's cortex which are maximally sensitive to the shape of a monkey's hand, or to monkey or human faces in various orientations; but the computations by means of which the brain recognizes such shapes are unknown—see Gross, Rocha-Miranda, & Bender, 1972; Perrett *et al.*, 1985.]

It may, then, be asked whether such a hypothesis irresponsibly begs the question at issue: namely, whether any causal mechanisms *can* be found underlying the "concepts" and "ideas" we attribute to persons, and accounting for their influence on behaviour. But the actual example of computers, which parallel logical or mathematical thought-processes to some extent, shows that it is not impossible for mechanistic systems to represent even highly abstract features of this sort. If information about external features (ranging from the finger-prints of some man to abstract logical relationships) can be somehow stored or represented in the machine, this representation may be referred to in any information-processing carried out by the machine that relates to the features in question. And the machine's overall performance will reflect the nature of its internal representations to some extent— as we shall see in more detail shortly. Psychologists are currently finding the concepts of information-theory and of cerebral modelling very useful in illuminating the control of behaviour— for example, in discussing the visual constancies and visual illusions, which have so far eluded explanation [Gregory, 1966; 1968]. Physiologists also use these concepts, in formulating questions about *what tasks* the nerve-cells are performing: though not much is known about which cells perform which task, and still less about how the cells are doing it.

The precise details of how the information is stored in any particular physical system are crucial questions for the cybernetics engineer, and also for the neurophysiologist insofar as he seeks to regard the brain as an information-processing system. But they are not crucial questions for the philosopher. Nor, importantly, are they crucial for the psychologist either. His prime concern is with the overall structure and control-features of behaviour, not with its physiological details. But it makes sense for him to suggest that the brain is an information-processing system that somehow models the environment (though we do not yet know exactly how), since physical systems—namely, computers—are already known which model or represent environmental features in a way that we fully understand.

V

These concepts of internal modelling and information processing can help in explaining the pathological behaviour that I described earlier, and are also relevant to intentional behaviour in general. To see how this is so, let us ask how we might attempt to simulate the motor aspects of a hysterical paralysis in a machine.

Suppose a computer built like a robot, with fingers and toes, upper and lower limbs, that can be flexed or extended just as human limbs can. The various wires carrying the electrical currents responsible for these movements are distributed on a plan paralleling that in human beings. For instance, the wires leading to the little finger and the outside half of the ring-finger are encased together within the same insulating tube; only when they reach the base of these fingers do they separate to go to their final destinations. With this robot we could simulate what I have called "simple" nervous injury, merely by cutting some wires. If we also provided a high-level switching mechanism in the head, we could simulate the temporary inhibition of particular nerve-groups that I mentioned before. But with the robot so far described we could *not* simulate the motor aspects of a hysterical paralysis.

Next we supply the robot's head with photo-electric cells, and attach variously coloured lights to different parts of its body; it will now be able to discriminate its own bodily movements at an elementary level. Finally, we add some negative feedback mechanism such that an incipient movement may be immediately inhibited by a message from the central core of the robot. This feedback mechanism can be "set" in different ways, so as to be activated for all and only those movements fulfilling certain criteria.

How must this mechanism be set so as to generate performance simulating a hysterical paralysis? By means of a system of coloured lights we can supply the robot with functional internal models, or simple "concepts" (or proto-concepts: only a more complex machine could possess real concepts [Boden, 1969]) of the parts of its body, which will correspond to the human layman's ideas rather than to those of the anatomist. For the layman, five of the fingers and one palm together form the unit "left hand", which is bounded by the wrist-joint. So all the coloured lights that are positioned on those parts are listed under one heading in the robot's memory-store; and the instruction "Stop movement" is associated with that list-heading in the program. Clearly, if the negative feedback mechanism is thus connected to the heading "left hand", the machine will show only incipient movements of any part of that hand; but it will be able to carry out other movements in a complete fashion.

If someone were to conclude from watching the behaviour that the wire, or wires, supplying electric pulses to the hand were damaged—or even temporarily switched off at some higher level—he would be wrong. We could not explain the robot's performance merely by talking about the distribution of wires to the hand, but should have to mention the *model* or *concept* of the "hand", instantiated in the core and connected to the negative feedback mechanism.

Of course, there must be some very complex causal (electronic) account underlying the account using the terminology of information-processing. (Likewise, there is, presumably, some complicated physiological mechanism determining the behaviour in the human case.) But we do not need to know exactly what this is, since for our purposes the most illuminating account is the one which stresses the (representational) *functions* of the physical processes concerned. Since the high-level control directing the performance is primarily directed to the list-heading "hand" (defined by the layman's visual criteria) rather than to the hand's mechanical components, it would be unhelpful merely to list the components affected. Similarly, it would be unhelpful merely to list the affected muscles in a true case of hysterical paralysis. To understand *why* the structure of the behaviour is as it is, we must refer to the concept of "hand" involved *even if* we know every mechanical detail. These details could be changed by engineers or surgeons, but the overall structure of behaviour would remain the same: the hand would still be paralysed. This is why the purely causal account is insufficient to explain behaviour even though it accurately lists all the physical factors determining the behaviour in a given case. Such an account fails to point out that many different cases of behaviour are all being directed by the same general model; the features of this model are reflected in the structure of behaviour, and explain its overall pattern.

Were we to build a group of robots, we could build into them (or program them so as to build up for themselves) somewhat different concepts, or models. Any robot that was not provided with an appropriate concept of "hand" just *could not* show the "paralytic" behaviour so far described, for no simple cutting or switching-off of any group of wires could effect such a result. The varying "paralyses" shown by different robots could be alleviated only by cancelling the instruction in the relevant robot's program (perhaps temporarily, as in hypnosis), not by tinkering with the limbs themselves.

If the robots had different internal models, their behaviour could not be explained purely in terms of laws about robots (or even *these* robots) *in general*—for instance, in terms of the generic blueprints of their electrical circuitry or of the principles of electronics. On the contrary, their behaviour could be fully explained (and successfully predicted) only by referring to the details of information-storage within each individual robot. This is the first step to regarding each individual robot as a different psychological *subject*, its behaviour varying from that of the other robots because of its *ideas* of particular *objects*; it is a first step to regarding the robot's behaviour as *intentional*.

(Of course it is only a first step: only a very much more complex behavioural system could merit the use of psychological predicates without scare-quotes. Moreover, these robots simulate only *some* of the features of a true hysterical paralysis. For example, the paralytic performance as described is arbitrary with respect to any of the machine's overall goals; but the clinical syndrome usually serves some purpose, such as defending the patient from certain traumatic situations. Charcot remarked that the aetiology of such cases was always sexual, but the Great War saw similar cases of "shell-shock" paralyses which clearly functioned as a protection from the front-line; such alternative defensive purposes are not represented in the simple robots I have described. Nor have I represented the unconscious, and seemingly involuntary, nature of the clinical cases; this might be done by varying the degree of interdependence and the availability of information-exchanges between the master-program and the various sub-programs. Again, the patient does not normally have to *look at* his limbs in order for the paralysis to occur, but presumably relies upon kinaesthetic information; this might be represented in a robot where information as to the start of any limb-movement was relayed to the master-program as a matter of course, and then monitored by it. In short, the thought-experiment described above concerns only the motor aspects of hysterical paralysis.)

VI

How does our imaginary robot relate to the logical criteria of intentionality suggested by Chisholm and others? It is characteristic of intentional propositions that their truth depends on psychological truths about the *subject* . It does not depend on nonpsychological facts about the object, even assuming that there *is* something in the physical world (what G. E. M. Anscombe [1965] terms the "material object") which can be sensibly identified as the object of thought in the case in question. In particular, the description under which the object is thought of by the subject is crucial.

It is this which suggests the application of intentional psychological predicates to the robots I have described, although such predicates can be understood only in a weak analogical sense when applied to robots as simple as these. For their behaviour is idea-dependent, being governed by the concepts or models embodied in each individual robot rather than by the environmental input directly. And the intentional features remarked upon by Chisholm are present in sentences describing the performance of these machines.

For example, consider the criterion of referential opacity. We can say of our robot that it is avoiding moving its left hand (inhibiting movement of the left hand), and that it is avoiding moving the fingers of that hand; but we cannot truly say that it is avoiding moving that part of its body which is made up of such-and-such metals in such-and-such a combination. For this information is nowhere stored (represented) inside the robot. And even if it were, we still could not say such a thing if this feature were not specifically connected to the negative feedback mechanism by the program, so that it acted as one of the criteria governing inhibition of movement. To say that the robot is avoiding moving these metallic components would be *untrue*, for it implies that the high-level control of its performance is directed to these components directly; whereas the control is in fact directed by more general ("visual") criteria defining *hand*. Thus the same performance would result if the components were rearranged, or replaced by others made of different metals.

Similarly, the indeterminacy of intentional statements remarked upon by W. Kneale [1968] could be exemplified if we gave the robot the instruction to raise a hand every ten minutes. Sometimes the left hand and sometimes the right hand would be raised, and either would fulfil the instruction. Whether the choice of hand were determined by some factor such as the current position of the limbs, or by regular alternation, or merely by a random operator, is irrelevant. Likewise, *any* cup of tea— weak or strong, Chinese or Indian—would satisfy the wish or demand for "a cup of tea".

Nonextensional occurrence would characterize phrases used in some sentences about our robot. For example, consider: "The robot at time $t - 1$ had the information that its foot was moving upwards". Granted that its foot was so moving at the time, we could not substitute any true expression in the above sentence *salve veritate* : we could not derive the truth of "The robot at time *t - 1* had the information that Socrates was a philosopher". Conversely, since in this sense the term "information" (like "opinion" and "belief") does not imply truth, we could sometimes say truly: "The robot at time *t - 2* had the information that its foot was not moving," even though this item of information was false. This state-of-affairs would occur, for instance, if the coloured lights failed. But we could not derive: "The robot at time *t - 2* had the information that Socrates was a greengrocer."

Again, from "The robot at time *t* had the information that its foot was moving," we can infer neither the truth nor the falsehood of the embedded clause, since we have no guarantee that the robot's mechanism was working properly at the time.

In general, any item of information stored in some system may be true or false. Its truth-value may depend primarily on some structural or mechanical feature of the system itself; or it may reflect the reliability of some other information-processing system (man or machine) which was the source of the item in question. Thus it follows that the simple sentence prefixes defined as intentional by Chisholm's two additional criteria include not only "John believes" and "John desires", but also "The robot has in memory-store the information that." Firstly, *every* sentence, whether it is itself contingent or not, is such that the result of prefixing it by this phrase is contingent [Chisholm, 1967, p. 203]. And secondly, Chisholm's more complex criterion could also be satisfied by our imaginary case. This criterion deals with the logical relations between the universally and existentially quantified forms of sentences into which intentional prefixes have been inserted [Chisholm, 1967, pp. 203-4; cf. Cohen, 1968, pp. 138-9]. For instance, the sentence, "John believes that, for every *x* , *x* is material" does not imply, "John believes that there exists an *x* such that *x* is material." But these relations could also hold of the equivalent sentences about the robot's information-store.

Of course, they need not hold—for we could construct the program such that the one sentence was always true, given the truth of the other. In those cases where these relations did hold, it would be irrelevant whether the set of sentences in question was specifically written into the basic program, or specifically provided as later input, or partially generated by the robot after a particular input-history. In like case, a man may be *told* that all unicorns are white, and that there are no unicorns; or he may *conclude* from illustrations that all unicorns are white, while keeping an open mind as to their existence. But these facts about the genesis of his beliefs are irrelevant to Chisholm's logical point, which is that a man might believe that all unicorns are white without believing that there are unicorns. Our robot might be programmed so as not to draw any existential inference from universally quantified propositions; in which case it could have the information that all unicorns are white, and yet not have the information that unicorns do exist.

Finally, consider the criterion of failure of existential generalization. Since a man may think of unicorns or search the skies for the planet Vulcan, neither of which exist, sentences containing the verbs *think of* and *search for* are intentional. So, too, are sentences stating some agent's purpose; for the end-state aimed at is always nonexistent insofar as it lies in the future, and is sometimes impossible of achievement (like squaring the circle). But our robot might be set to aim at a certain goal, which goal could direct its activity in various ways; and the goal might never be reached , for any one of a number of reasons. For instance, we might give the instruction: "Touch left elbow with fingers of left hand." This would result in some movements, for the robot could move its fingers *nearer* to its left elbow than they had been before. But let us hope that it has been provided with some automatic stop-rule, so that it does not go on aiming at this unattainable goal for the rest of its days.

This latter example would probably not convince R. Taylor, who in his discussion of mechanism and purpose [Taylor, 1966] has derided "the folly of speaking of machines as purposeful or goal-directed beings." He says [pp. 238-239]:

> An astronomer might search with his glass for the planet Vulcan, but no sense can be made of the idea of an automatic, self-guiding and self-adjusting telescope, of

whatever complexity or elaborate design, undertaking a search of the skies for that planet; for no such planet exists.... There is no difference between two self-operating telescopes, one of which is designed to "search" the skies endlessly, stopping at nothing, and the other of which is designed to "search" the skies, stopping only if it chances upon the planet Vulcan.

It is true that there might be no difference in overt performance between these two telescopes, despite the difference in the minds of the designers. Similarly, our robot "trying" to touch its elbow would perform the very same movements as one "set" merely to flex the relevant joints maximally. And a quality-control machine in a canning factory would show the same performance if it was set to reject only overweight cans, as if it were set to reject underweight cans also but there happened to be no underweight cans on the conveyer belt. In all of these cases the overt performance could be generated in the absence of any internal models, and might not seem to require explanation in terms of anything analogous to a "purpose".

But this is not the case if we consider a slightly more complex example. Suppose a robot built for manual library-retrieval: it can move along the lanes between the shelves, read the titles on the spines, pick out a book from its place on the shelf, and deposit it in the operator's briefcase. We give it the instruction: "Find *The Spy Who Came In From The Cold,* by Ian Fleming." Accordingly, it looks for this item in the author-catalogue, to find its detailed shelf-mark. Not surprisingly, it does not find it—for there is no such book. However, it allows for the contingency that the catalogue-entry may be missing, and commences a physical search for the book. It sets its search-mechanism to "*F* ", and moves along the lanes until it comes to the *F* section. Now it sets its mechanism to "Fleming", and moves accordingly; it ignores *George Fleming* , moving on to *Ian Fleming* ; it moves up and down the *Ian Fleming* section (perhaps pausing in front of *The Spy Who Worried,* if we allow ourselves to posit this hypothetical Flemming work); after ten minutes with no success, it returns to the catalogue room. At this point it may give up. Or, like some human beings in a comparable situation, it might allow for the possibility of a faulty instruction: thus it may now search the title catalogue, and find the entry for *The Spy Who Came In From The Cold*, by John Le Carré. Accordingly, it goes to the relevant shelf-mark, takes the book, and delivers it to the operator with the typed out message: "Was instruction faulty?"

This performance is very different indeed from that of a robot designed "to search [the library] endlessly, stopping at nothing." Moreover, it could be made fully intelligible (and its performance reliably predicted) only by mentioning the instructions and search-rules controlling the performance, including the criteria for recognition of the book and the subroutines to be brought into play given certain kinds of failure. A purely causal account could in principle be given by an all-seeing engineer, but this would not be sufficient to describe or explain what was *really* going on. (This remains true even though in this case we could probably explain the whole episode in terms of the *operator's* predilections for bedtime reading. Whether the robot accepts a goal from this Svengali-figure, or generates it itself in the course of its operation, is irrelevant to the main point.)

VII

In sum: those philosophers who have claimed that irreducibly intentional accounts are necessary to the explanation of behaviour are correct. But this fact does not constitute a threat to "the unity of science" in any way.

We must suppose that behaviour is largely mediated and controlled by means of internal—and often idiosyncratic—representations of the environment, rather than by the environment directly. Being mediated by them, behaviour will naturally reflect their features as well as environmental conditions. It is this which accounts for the intentional characteristics of behaviour, and which underlies the logical features remarked upon by Chisholm and others. Those who have stressed the close relationship between intentionality and intensionality [e.g. Kneale, 1968] are concerned to emphasize those cases where the "representation" involved is a *verbal* form of thought. Explanation of behaviour must include reference to these internal models, and to the general structure of the information-processing going on within the system, whether organism or computer. Description of the control functions of the system will include reference to its perceptual classifications (which may sometimes be faulty); to its hypotheses and beliefs (which may sometimes be false); to the tricks and heuristics on which it relies in situations of difficulty (which may mislead it); and to its goals and purposes (which may be unachievable). This is why the use of one intentional term involves us in the use of others [cf. Chisholm, 1957, ch. 11].

A causal account, although in a sense fully *complete*, cannot be fully *adequate*, for it cannot exhibit these structural features. So Taylor [1966, p. 229] is mistaken when he claims that "An engineer of suitable training can describe and explain the mechanics of [guided missiles and all 'goal-directed' machines] without needing any concepts whatever except those of physical science, and in particular, he can give a *complete* and adequate explanation without once introducing the idea of purpose or goal" (italics in original)—unless we interpret his word "mechanics" so narrowly that it excludes all those structural features of the machine's behaviour which lead one to use words like "goal" or "purpose" in the first place.

In spite of (human) behaviour which we most naturally explain in terms of "the mind controlling the body," we need not abandon hope of a purely physicalist neurophysiology, accounting for behaviour at the causal level. It is not a special type of cause (nor any type of causelessness), but a particular type of physical *organization*, which allows us to speak of behaviour as being directed by thoughts of non-existent objects and by purposes impossible of achievement.

Chapter 6

Escaping from the Chinese Room

John Searle, in his paper on "Minds, Brains, and Programs" [1980], argues that computational theories in psychology are essentially worthless. He makes two main claims: that computational theories, being purely formal in nature, cannot possibly help us to understand mental processes; and that computer hardware—unlike neuroprotein—obviously lacks the right causal powers to generate mental processes. I shall argue that both these claims are mistaken.

His first claim takes for granted the widely-held (formalist) assumption that the "computations" studied in computer science are purely syntactic, that they can be defined (in terms equally suited to symbolic logic) as *the formal manipulation of abstract symbols, by the application of formal rules* . It follows, he says, that formalist accounts—appropriate in explaining the meaningless "information"-processing or "symbol"-manipulations in computers—are unable to explain how human minds employ *information* or *symbols* properly so-called. Meaning, or intentionality, cannot be explained in computational terms.

Searle's point here is not that no machine can think. Humans can think, and humans—he allows—are machines; he even adopts the materialist credo that only machines can think. Nor is he saying that humans and programs are utterly incommensurable. He grants that, at some highly abstract level of description, people (like everything else) are instantiations of digital computers. His point, rather, is that nothing can think, mean, or understand *solely* in virtue of its instantiating a computer program.

To persuade us of this, Searle employs an ingenious thought-experiment. He imagines himself locked in a room, in which there are various slips of paper with doodles on them; a window through which people can pass further doodle-papers to him, and through which he can pass papers out; and a book of rules (in English) telling him how to pair the doodles, which are always identified by their shape, or form. Searle spends his time, while inside the room, manipulating the doodles according to the rules.

One rule, for example, instructs him that when *squiggle-squiggle* is passed in to him, he should give out *squoggle-squoggle* . The rule-book also provides for more complex sequences of doodle-pairing, where only the first and last steps mention the transfer of paper into or out of the room. Before finding any rule directly instructing him to give out a slip of paper, he may have to locate a *blongle* doodle and compare it with a *blungle* doodle—in which case, it is the result of this comparison which determines the nature of the doodle he passes out. Sometimes, many such doodle-doodle comparisons, and consequent doodle-selections, have to be made by him inside the room before he finds a rule allowing him to pass anything out.

So far as Searle-in-the-room is concerned, the *squiggles* and *squoggles* are mere meaningless doodles. Unknown to him, however, they are Chinese characters. The people outside the room, being Chinese, interpret them as such. Moreover, the patterns passed in and out at the window are understood by them as *questions* and *answers* respectively: the rules happen to be such that most of the questions are paired, either directly or indirectly, with what they recognize as a sensible answer. But Searle himself (inside the room) knows nothing of this.

The point, says Searle, is that Searle-in-the-room is clearly instantiating a computer program. That is, he is performing purely formal manipulations of uninterpreted patterns: he is all syntax, and no semantics.

The doodle-pairing rules are equivalent to the IF-THEN rules, or "productions", commonly used (for example) in expert systems. Some of the internal doodle-comparisons could be equivalent to what AI-workers in natural-language processing call a script—for instance, the restaurant script described by R. C. Schank and R. P. Abelson [1977]. In that case, Searle-in-the-room's paper-passing performance would be essentially comparable to the performance of a "question-answering" Schankian text-analysis program. But "question-answering" is not question-answering. Searle-in-the-room is not really *answering* : how could he, since he cannot understand the questions? Practice does not help (except perhaps in making the doodle-pairing swifter): if Searle-in-the-room ever escapes, he will be just as ignorant of Chinese as he was when he was first locked in.

Certainly, the Chinese people outside might find it useful to keep Searle-in-the-room fed and watered, much as in real life we are willing to spend large sums of money on computerized "advice" systems. But the fact that people who *already* possess understanding may use an intrinsically meaningless formalist computational system to provide what they interpret (*sic*) as questions, answers, designations, interpretations, or symbols is irrelevant. They can do this only if they can externally specify a mapping between the formalism and matters of interest to them. In principle, one and the same formalism might be mappable onto several different domains, so could be used (by people) in answering questions about any of those domains. In itself, however, it would be meaningless—as are the Chinese symbols from the point of view of Searle-in-the-room.

It follows, Searle argues, that no system can understand anything solely in virtue of its instantiating a computer program. For if it could, then Searle-in-the-room would understand Chinese. Hence, theoretical psychology cannot properly be grounded in computational concepts.

Searle's second claim concerns what a proper explanation of understanding would be like. According to him, it would acknowledge that meaningful symbols must be embodied in something having "the right causal powers" for generating understanding, or intentionality. Obviously, he says, brains do have such causal powers whereas computers do not. More precisely (since the brain's organization could be paralleled in a computer), neuroprotein does whereas metal and silicon do not: the bio-chemical properties of the brain-matter are crucial.

A. Newell's [1980] widely-cited definition of "physical symbol systems" is rejected by Searle, because it demands merely that symbols be embodied in some material that can implement formalist computations—which computers, admittedly, can do. On Searle's view, no electronic computer can really manipulate symbols, nor really designate or interpret anything at all—*irrespective* of any causal dependencies linking its internal physi-cal patterns to its behaviour. (This strongly realist view of inten-tionality contrasts with the instrumentalism of D. C. Dennett [1971]. For Dennett, an intentional system is one whose behavi-our we can explain, predict, and control only by ascribing belief, goals, and rationality to it. On this criterion, some *existing* com-puter programs are intentional systems, and the hypothetical humanoids beloved of science-fiction would be intentional systems *a fortiori*.)

Intentionality, Searle declares, is a biological phenomenon. As such, it is just as dependent on the underlying biochemistry as are photosynthesis and lactation. He grants that neuroprotein may not be the only substance in the universe capable of supporting mental life, much as substances other than chlorophyll may be able (on Mars, perhaps) to catalyse the synthesis of carbohy-drates. But he rejects metal or silicon as potential alternatives, even on Mars. He asks whether a computer made out of old beer cans could possibly *understand*—a rhetorical question to which the expected answer is a resounding "No!" In short, Searle takes it to be intuitively obvious that the inorganic substances with which (today's) computers are manufactured are essentially in-capable of supporting mental functions.

In assessing Searle's two-pronged critique of computational psychology, let us first consider his view that intentionality must be biologically grounded. One might be tempted to call this a "positive" claim, in contrast with his (negative) claim that purely formalist theories cannot explain mentality. However, this would be to grant it more than it deserves, for its explanatory power is illusory. The biological analogies mentioned by Searle

are misleading, and the intuitions to which he appeals are un-
reliable.

The brain's production of intentionality, we are told, is comparable to photosynthesis—but is it, really? We can define the
products of photosynthesis, clearly distinguishing various sugars
and starches within the general class of carbohydrates, and
showing how these differ from other biochemical products such
as proteins. Moreover, we not only *know that* chlorophyll
supports photosynthesis, we also *understand how* it does so (and
why various other chemicals cannot). We know that it is a catalyst
rather than a "raw material"; and we can specify the point at
which, and the sub-atomic process by which, its catalytic function is exercised. With respect to brains and understanding, the
case is very different.

Our theory of what intentionality is (never mind how it is
generated) does not bear comparison with our knowledge of
carbohydrates: just what intentionality *is* , is still philosophically
controversial. We cannot even be entirely confident that we can
recognize it when we see it. It is generally agreed that the
propositional attitudes are intentional, and that feelings and
sensations are not; but there is no clear consensus about the
intentionality of emotions.

Various attempts have been made to characterize intentionality, and to distinguish its sub-species as distinct intentional states
(beliefs , desires, hopes, intentions, and the like). Searle himself
has made a number of relevant contributions, from his early work
on speech-acts [1969] to his more recent account [1983] of intentionality in general. A commonly used criterion (adopted by
Brentano in the nineteenth century and also by Searle) is a
psychological one. In Brentano's words, intentional states direct
the mind on an object; in Searle's, they have intrinsic representational capacity, or "aboutness"; in either case they relate the
mind to the world, and to possible worlds. But some writers
define intentionality in *logical* terms [Chisholm, 1967]. It is not
even clear whether the logical and psychological definitions are
precisely co-extensive [Boden, 1970]. In brief, no theory of
intentionality is accepted as unproblematic, as the chemistry of
carbohydrates is.

As for the brain's biochemical "synthesis" of intentionality, this is even more mysterious. We have very good reason to believe *that* neuroprotein supports intentionality, but we have hardly any idea *how*—*qua* neuroprotein—it is able to do so. Insofar as we understand these matters at all, we focus on the neurochemical basis of certain *informational functions*—such as message-passing, facilitation, and inhibition—embodied in neurones and synapses. For example: how the sodium-pump at the cell membrane enables an action potential to propagate along the axon; how electrochemical changes cause a neurone to enter into and recover from its refractory period; or how neuronal thresholds can be altered by neurotransmitters, such as acetylcholine.

With respect to a visual cell, for instance, a crucial psychological question may be *whether it can function so as to detect intensity-gradients.* If the neurophysiologist can tell us which molecules enable it to do so, so much the better. But from the psychological point of view, it is not the biochemistry as such which matters but the information-bearing functions grounded in it. (Searle apparently admits this, when he says, "The type of realizations that intentional states have in the brain may be describable at a much higher functional level than that of the specific biochemistry of the neurons involved" [1983, p. 272].)

As work in "computer vision" has shown, metal and silicon are undoubtedly able to support some of the functions necessary for the 2D-to-3D mapping involved in vision. Moreover they can embody specific mathematical functions for recognizing intensity-gradients (namely "DOG-detectors", which compute differences of Gaussians) which seem to be involved in many biological visual systems. Admittedly, it may be that metal and silicon cannot support all the functions involved in normal vision, or in understanding generally. Perhaps only neuroprotein can do so, so that only creatures with a "terrestrial" biology can enjoy intentionality. But we have no specific reason, at present, to think so. Most important in this context, any such reasons we might have in the future must be grounded in empirical discovery: intuitions will not help.

If one asks which mind-matter dependencies are intuitively plausible, the answer must be that *none* is. Nobody who was puzzled about intentionality (as opposed to action potentials) ever exclaimed "Sodium—of course!" Sodium-pumps are no less "obviously" absurd than silicon chips, electrical polarities no less "obviously" irrelevant than old beer cans, acetylcholine hardly less surprising than beer. The fact that the first member of each of these three pairs is *scientifically* compelling does not make any of them *intuitively* intelligible: our initial surprise persists.

Our intuitions might change, with the advance of science. Possibly we shall eventually see neuroprotein (and perhaps silicon too) as obviously capable of embodying mind, much as we now see biochemical substances in general (including chlorophyll) as obviously capable of producing other such substances— an intuition that was not obvious, even to chemists, prior to the synthesis of urea. At present, however, our intuitions have nothing useful to say about the material basis of intentionality. Searle's "positive" claim, his putative alternative explanation of intentionality, is at best a promissory note, at worst mere mystery-mongering.

Searle's negative claim—that formal-computational theories cannot explain understanding—is less quickly rebutted. My rebuttal will involve two parts: the first directly addressing his example of the Chinese room, the second dealing with his background assumption (on which his example depends) that computer programs are pure syntax.

The Chinese room example has engendered much debate, both within and outside the community of cognitive science. Some criticisms were anticipated by Searle himself in his original paper, others appeared as the accompanying peer-commentary (together with his Reply), and more have been published since. Here, I shall concentrate on only two points: what Searle calls the Robot reply, and what I shall call the English reply.

The Robot reply accepts that the only understanding of Chinese which exists in Searle's example is that enjoyed by the Chinese people outside the room. Searle-in-the-room's inability to connect Chinese characters with events in the outside world shows that he does not understand Chinese. Likewise, a Schankian teletyping computer that cannot recognize a restaurant, hand money to a waiter, or chew a morsel of food understands nothing of restaurants—even if it can usefully "answer" our questions about them. But a robot provided not only with a restaurant-script but also with camera-fed visual programs and limbs capable of walking and picking things up, would be another matter. If the input-output behaviour of such a robot were identical with that of human beings, then it would demonstrably understand both restaurants and the natural language—Chinese, perhaps—used by people to communicate with it.

Searle's first response to the Robot reply is to claim a victory already, since the reply concedes that cognition is not solely a matter of formal symbol-manipulation but requires in addition a set of causal relations with the outside world. Second, Searle insists that to add perceptuomotor capacities to a computational system is not to add intentionality, or understanding.

He argues this point by imagining a robot which, instead of being provided with a computer program to make it work, has a miniaturized Searle inside it—in its skull, perhaps. Searle-in-the-robot, with the aid of a (new) rule book, shuffles paper and passes *squiggles* and *squoggles* in and out, much as Searle-in-the-room did before him. But now, some or all of the incoming Chinese characters are not handed in by Chinese people, but are triggered by causal processes in the cameras and audio-equipment in the robot's eyes and ears. And the outgoing Chinese characters are not received by Chinese hands, but by motors and levers attached to the robot's limbs—which are caused to move as a result. In short, this robot is apparently able not only to answer questions in Chinese, but also to see and do things accordingly: it can recognize raw bean sprouts and, if the recipe requires it, toss them into a wok as well as the rest of us.

(The work on computer vision mentioned above suggests that the vocabulary of Chinese would require considerable extension for this example to be carried through. And the large body of AI-research on language-processing suggests that the same could be said of the English required to express the rules in Searle's initial "question-answering" example. In either case, what Searle-in-the-room needs is not so much Chinese, or even English, as a programming language. We shall return to this point presently.) Like his roombound predecessor, however, Searle-in-the-robot knows nothing of the wider context. He is just as ignorant of Chinese as he ever was, and has no more purchase of the outside world than he did in the original example. To him, bean-sprouts and woks are invisible and intangible: all Searle-in-the-robot can see and touch, besides the rule-book and the doodles, are his own body and the inside walls of the robot's skull. Consequently, Searle argues, the robot cannot be credited with understanding of any of these worldly matters. In truth, it is not *seeing* or *doing* anything at all: it is "simply moving about as a result of its electrical wiring and its program," which latter is instantiated by the man inside it, who "has no intentional states of the relevant type" [1980, p. 420].

Searle's argument here is unacceptable as a rebuttal of the Robot reply, because it draws a false analogy between the imagined example and what is claimed by computational psychology.

Searle-in-the-robot is supposed by Searle to be performing the functions performed (according to computational theories) by the human brain. But, whereas most computationalists do not ascribe intentionality to the brain (and those who do, as we shall see presently, do so only in a very limited way), Searle characterizes Searle-in-the-robot as enjoying full-blooded intentionality, just as he does himself. Computational psychology does not credit the brain with *seeing beansprouts* or *understanding English*: intentional states such as these are properties of people, not of brains. In general, although representations and mental processes are assumed (by computationalists and Searle alike) to be embodied in the brain, the sensorimotor capacities and propositional attitudes which they make possible are ascribed to the person as a whole. So Searle's description of the system inside the robot's skull as one which can understand English does not truly parallel what computationalists say about the brain.

Indeed, the specific procedures hypothesized by computational psychologists, and embodied by them in computer models of the mind, are relatively stupid—and they become more and more stupid as one moves to increasingly basic theoretical levels. Consider theories of natural-language parsing, for example. A parsing-procedure that searches for a determiner does not understand English, and nor does a procedure for locating the reference of a personal pronoun: only the person whose brain performs these interpretative processes, and many others associated with them, can do that. The capacity to understand English involves a host of interacting information-processes, each of which performs only a very limited function but which together provide the capacity to take English sentences as input and give appropriate English sentences as output. Similar remarks apply to the individual components of computational theories of vision, problem-solving, or learning.   Precisely because psychologists wish to *explain* human language, vision, reasoning, and learning, they posit underlying processes which lack these capacities.

In short, Searle's description of the robot's pseudo-brain (that is, of Searle-in-the-robot) as understanding English involves a category-mistake comparable to treating the brain as the bearer—as opposed to the causal basis—of intelligence.

Someone might object here that I have contradicted myself, that I am claiming that one cannot ascribe intentionality to brains and yet am implicitly doing just that. For I spoke of the brain's effecting "stupid" component procedures—but stupidity is virtually a *species* of intelligence. To be stupid is to be intelligent, but not very (a person or a fish can be stupid, but a stone or a river cannot).

My defense would be twofold. First, the most basic theoretical level of all would be at the neuroscientific equivalent of the machine code, a level "engineered" by evolution. The facts that a certain light-sensitive cell *can* respond to intensity-gradients by acting as a DOG-detector and that one neurone *can* inhibit the firing of another, are explicable by the biochemistry of the brain. The notion of stupidity, even in scare-quotes, is wholly inappropriate in discussing such facts. However, these very basic infor-mation-processing functions (DOG-detecting and synaptic inhibition) *could* properly be described as "very, very, very... stupid". This of course implies that intentional language, if only of a highly grudging and uncomplimentary type, is applicable to brain-processes after all—which prompts the second point in my defence. I did not say that intentionality cannot be ascribed to brains, but that full-blooded intentionality cannot. Nor did I say that brains cannot understand anything at all, in howsoever limited a fashion, but that they cannot (for example) understand English. I even hinted, several paragraphs ago, that a few computationalists do ascribe some degree of intentionality to the brain (or to the computational processes going on in the brain). These two points will be less obscure after we have considered the "English" reply and its bearing on Searle's background assumption that formal-syntactic computational theories are purely syntactic.

The crux of the English reply is that the instantiation of a computer program, whether by man or by manufactured machine, does involve understanding—at least of the rule-book. Searle's initial example depends critically on Searle-in-the-room's being able to understand the language in which the rules are written, namely English; similarly, without Searle-in-the-robot's familiarity with English, the robot's bean-sprouts would never get thrown into the wok. Moreover, as remarked above, the vocabulary of English (and, for Searle-in-the-robot, of Chinese too) would have to be significantly modified to make the example work.

An unknown language (whether Chinese or Linear B) can be dealt with only as an aesthetic object or a set of systematically related forms. Artificial languages can be designed and studied, by the logician or the pure mathematician, with only their structural properties in mind (although D. R. Hofstadter's [1979] example of the quasi-arithmetical MU-game shows that a psychologically compelling, and predictable, interpretation of a formal calculus may arise spontaneously). But one normally responds in a very different way to the symbols of one's native tongue; indeed, it is very difficult to "bracket" (ignore) the meanings of familiar words. The view held by computational psychologists, that natural languages can be characterized in procedural terms, is relevant here: words, clauses, and sentences can be seen as mini-programs. The symbols in a natural language one understands initiate mental activity of various kinds. To learn a language is to set up the relevant causal connections, not only between words and the world ("cat" and the thing on the mat) but between words and the many non-introspectible procedures involved in interpreting them.

Moreover, we do not need to be told *ex hypothesi* (by Searle) that Searle-in-the-room understands English: his behaviour while in the room shows clearly that he does. Or, rather, it shows that he understands a *highly limited subset* of English.

Searle-in-the-room could be suffering form total amnesia with respect to 99% of Searle's English vocabulary, and it would make no difference. The only grasp of English he needs is whatever is necessary to interpret (*sic*) the rule-book—which specifies how to accept, select, compare, and give out different patterns. Unlike Searle, Searle-in-the-room does not require words like "catalyse", "beer-can", "chlorophyll", and "restaurant". But he may need "find", "compare", "two", "triangular", and "window" (although his understanding of these words could be much less full than Searle's). He must understand conditional sentences, if any rule states that if he sees a *squoggle* he should give out a *squiggle* . Very likely, he must understand some way of expressing negation, temporal ordering, and (especially if he is to learn to do his job faster) generalization. If the rules he uses include some which parse the Chinese sentences, then he will need words for grammatical categories too. (He will not need explicit rules for parsing English sentences, such as the parsing-procedures employed in AI-programs for language-processing, because he already understands English.)

In short, Searle-in-the-room needs to understand only that subset of Searle's English which is equivalent to the programming language understood by a computer generating the same "question-answering" input-output behaviour at the window. Similarly, Searle-in-the-robot must be able to understand whatever subset of English is equivalent to the programming language understood by a fully computerised visuomotor robot.

The two preceding sentences may seem to beg the very question at issue. Indeed, to speak thus of the programming language understood by a computer is seemingly self-contradictory. For Searle's basic premise—which he assumes is accepted by all participants in the debate—is that a computer program is purely formal in nature: the computation it specifies is purely syntactic, and has no intrinsic meaning or semantic content to be understood.

If we accept this premise, the English reply sketched above can be dismissed forthwith, for seeking to draw a parallel where no parallel can properly be drawn. But if we do not, if—*pace* Searle (and others [Fodor, 1980; Stitch, 1983])—computer programs are not concerned only with syntax, then the English reply might be relevant after all. We must now turn to address this basic question.

Certainly, one can for certain purposes think of a computer program as an uninterpreted logical calculus. For example, one might be able to prove, by purely formal means, that a particular well-formed-formula is derivable from the program's data-structures and inferential rules. Moreover, it is true that a so-called interpreter program that could take as input the list-structure "(FATHER (MAGGIE))" and return "(LEONARD)" would do so on formal criteria alone, having no way of interpreting these patterns as possibly denoting real people. Likewise, as Searle points out, programs provided with restaurant-scripts are not thereby provided with knowledge of restaurants. The existence of a mapping between a formalism and a certain domain does not in itself provide the manipulator of the formalism with any understanding of that domain.

But what must not be forgotten is that a computer program is *a program for a computer* : when a program is run on suitable hardware, the machine *does* something as a result (hence the use in computer science of the words "instruction" and "obey"). At the level of the machine code the effect of the program on the computer is direct, because the machine is engineered so that a given instruction elicits a unique operation (instructions in high-level languages must be converted into machine-code instructions before they can be obeyed). A programmed instruction, then, is not a mere formal pattern—nor even a declarative statement (although it may for some purposes be though of under either of those descriptions). It is a procedure-specification that, given a suitable hardware-context, can cause the procedure in question to be executed.

One might put this by saying that a programming language is a medium not only for expressing *representations* (structures that can be written on a page or provided to a computer, some of which structures may be isomorphic with things that interest people) but also for bringing about the *representational activity* of certain machines.

One might even say that a representation *is* an activity rather than a structure. Many philosophers and psychologists have supposed that mental representations are intrinsically active. Among those who have recently argued for this view is Hofstadter [1985], who specifically criticizes Newell's account of *symbols* as manipulable formal tokens. In his words, "the brain itself does not 'manipulate symbols'; the brain is the medium in which the symbols are floating and in which they trigger each other" [p. 648]. Hofstadter expresses more sympathy for "connectionist" than for "formalist" psychological theories. Connectionist approaches involve parallel-processing systems broadly reminiscent of the brain, and are well suited to model cerebral representations, symbols, or concepts, as *dynamic* . But it is not only connectionists who can view concepts as intrinsically active, and not only *cerebral* representations which can be thought of in this way: this claim has been generalized to cover traditional computer programs, specifically designed for von Neumann machines. The computer scientist B. C. Smith [1982] argues that programmed representations, too, are inherently active—and that an adequate theory of the semantics of programming languages would recognize the fact.

At present, Smith claims, computer scientists have a radically inadequate understanding of such matters. He reminds us that, as remarked above, there is no general agreement—either within or outside computer science—about what *intentionality* is, and deep unclarities about *representation* as well. Nor can unclarities be avoided by speaking more technically, in terms of *computation* and *formal symbol manipulation* . For the computer scientist's understanding of what these phenomena really are is also largely intuitive. Smith's discussion of programming languages identifies some fundamental confusions within computer science. Especially relevant here is his claim that computer scientists commonly make too complete a theoretical separation between a program's control-functions and its nature as a formal-syntactic system.

The theoretical divide criticized by Smith is evident in the widespread "dual calculus" approach to programming. The dual calculus approach posits a sharp theoretical distinction between a declarative (or denotational) representational structure and the procedural language that interprets it when the program is run. Indeed, the knowledge representation and the interpreter are sometimes written in two quite distinct formalisms (such as the predicate calculus and LISP, respectively). Often, however, they are both expressed in the same formalism; for example, LISP (an acronym for LISt-Processing language) allows facts and procedures to be expressed in formally similar ways, and so does PROLOG (PROgramming-in-LOGic). In such cases the dual calculus approach dictates that the (single) programming-language concerned be theoretically described in two quite different ways.

To illustrate the distinction at issue here, suppose that we wanted a representation of family relationships, which could be used to provide answers to questions about such matters. We might decide to employ a list-structure to represent such facts as that Leonard is the father of Maggie. Or we might prefer a frame-based representation, in which the relevant name-slots in the FATHER-frame could be simultaneously filled by "LEONARD" and "MAGGIE". Again, we might choose a formula of the predicate calculus, saying that there exist two people (namely, Leonard and Maggie), and Leonard is the father of Maggie. Last, we might employ the English sentence "Leonard is the father of Maggie."

Each of these four representations could be written/drawn on paper (as are the rules in the rule-book used by Searle-in-the-room), for us to interpret *if* we have learnt how to handle the relevant notation. Alternatively, they could be embodied in a computer data-base. But to make them usable by the computer, there has to be an interpreter-program which (for instance) can find the item "LEONARD" when we "ask" it who is the father of Maggie. No-one with any sense would embody list-structures in a computer without providing it also with a *list-processing* facility, nor give it frames without a *slot-filling* mechanism, logical formulae without *rules of inference* , or English sentences without *parsing-procedures* . (Analogously, people who knew that Searle speaks no Portuguese would not give Searle-in-the-room a Portuguese rule-book, unless they were prepared to teach him the language first.)

Smith does not deny that there is an important distinction between the *denotational import* of an expression (broadly: what actual or possible worlds can be mapped onto it) and its *procedural consequence* (broadly: what it does, or makes happen). The fact that the expression "(FATHER (MAGGIE))" is isomorphic with a certain parental relationship between two actual people (and so might be mapped onto that relationship by us) is one thing. The fact that the expression "(FATHER (MAGGIE))" can cause a certain computer to locate "LEONARD" is quite another thing. Were it not so, the dual calculus approach would not have developed. But he argues that, rather than persisting with the dual calculus approach, it would be more elegant and less confusing to adopt a "unified" theory of programming languages, designed to cover both denotative and procedural aspects.

He shows that many basic terms on either side of the dual-calculus divide have deep theoretical commonalities as well as significant differences. The notion of *variable*, for instance, is understood in somewhat similar fashion by the logician and the computer scientist: both allow that a variable can have different *values* assigned to it at different times. That being so, it is redundant to have two distinct theories of what a variable is. To some extent, however, logicians and computer scientists understand different things by this term: the value of a variable in the LISP programming language (for example) is another LISP-expression, whereas the value of a variable in logic is usually some object external to the formalism itself. These differences should be clarified—not least to avoid confusion when a system attempts to reason *about* variables by *using* variables. In short, we need a single definition of "variable", allowing both for its declarative use (in logic) and for its procedural use (in programming). Having shown that similar remarks apply to other basic computational terms, Smith outlines a unitary account of the semantics of LISP and describes a new calculus ("MANTIQ") designed with the unified approach in mind.

As the example of using variables to reason about variables suggests, a unified theory of computation could illuminate how *reflective* knowledge is possible. For, given such a theory, a system's representations of data and of processes—including processes internal to the system itself—would be essentially comparable. This theoretical advantage has psychological relevance (and was a major motivation behind Smith's work).

For our present purpose, however, the crucial point is that a fundamental theory of *programs*, and of *computation*, should acknowledge that an essential function of a computer program is to make things happen. Whereas symbolic logic can be viewed as mere playing around with uninterpreted formal calculi (such as the predicate calculus), and computational logic can be seen as the study of abstract timeless relations in mathematically specified "machines" (such as Turing machines), computer science cannot properly be described in either of these ways.

It follows from Smith's argument that the familiar characterization of computer programs as all syntax and no semantics is mistaken. The inherent procedural consequences of any computer program give it a toehold in semantics, where the semantics in question is not denotational, but causal. The analogy is with Searle-in-the-room's understanding of English, not his understanding of Chinese.

This is implied also by A. Sloman's [1986a; 1986b] discussion of the sense in which programmed instructions and computer-symbols must be thought of as having some semantics, howsoever restricted. In a causal semantics, the meaning of a symbol (whether simple or complex) is to be sought by reference to its causal links with other phenomena. The central questions are "What causes the symbol to be built and/or activated?" and "What happens as a result of it?" The answers will sometimes mention external objects and events visible to an observer, and sometimes they will not.

If the system is a human, animal, or robot, it may have causal powers which enable it to refer to restaurants and bean-sprouts (the philosophical complexities of reference to external, including unobservable, objects may be ignored here, but are helpfully discussed by Sloman). But whatever the information-processing system concerned, the answers will sometimes describe purely *internal* computational processes—whereby other symbols are built, other instructions activated. Examples include the interpretative processes inside Searle-in-the-room's mind (comparable perhaps to the parsing and semantic procedures defined for automatic natural-language processing) that are elicited by English words, and the computational processes within a Schankian text-analysis program. Although such a program cannot use the symbol "restaurant" to mean *restaurant* (because it has no causal links with restaurants, food, and so forth), its internal symbols and procedures do embody some minimal understanding of certain other matters—of what it is to compare two formal structures, for example.

One may feel that the "understanding" involved in such a case is *so* minimal that this word should not be used at all. So be it. As Sloman makes clear, the important question is not *"When does a machine understand something?"* (a question which misleadingly implies that there is some clear cut-off point at which understanding ceases) but *"What things does a machine (whether biological or not) need to be able to do in order to be able to understand?"* This question is relevant not only to the *possibility* of a computational psychology, but to its *content* also.

In sum, my discussion has shown Searle's attack on computational psychology to be ill-founded. To view Searle-in-the-room as an instantiation of a computer program is not to say that he lacks all understanding. Since the theories of a formalist-computational psychology should be likened to computer programs rather than to formal logic, computational psychology is not in principle incapable of explaining how meaning attaches to mental processes.

Chapter 7
Is Equilibration Important?

Introduction

Piaget described equilibration as a "development factor" of fundamental psychological importance, more general even than heredity, environment, or social education, since "it intervenes in every hereditary or acquired process, and intervenes in their interactions" [Piaget, 1958, p.836]. He believed his account of equilibration not only to be of great value to psychology, but also to have the potential to unify developmental psychology, theoretical biology, sociology, and epistemology. Although I shall challenge these assumptions, claiming that they must be rejected in their strong form, I shall argue that an important theoretical problem is marked (though neither clearly expressed nor solved) by the vocabulary of equilibration.

By "equilibration", Piaget meant an adaptive interaction (consisting of simultaneous assimilation and accommodation) such that overall integration of the self-adapting system is maintained throughout any structural development taking place [*ibid*.]. He described it as carrying the system from a state of "disequilibrium" to one of relative "equilibrium", meaning that the failure of the system in its earlier form to make appropriate (assimilatory and/or accommodatory) adjustments initiates a self-development such that in its later form its powers are adequate to meet new situational demands. It is because self-adapting systems are characteristic of life, whether at the biological or the psychological level, that Piaget hoped for an interdisciplinary unification in terms of a general theory of equilibration.

Many committed Piagetians regard this concept as Piaget's prime contribution to psychology. Such people use his terminology of equilibration and repeat his claims about it as though the former were crystal clear, the latter evidently true, and their union genuinely explanatory. However, even an admirer of Piaget has dismissed the concept as "surplus baggage", contributing nothing useful to theory or experimental design [Bruner, 1959, p. 365]. And hostile critics express especial exasperation at this use of polysyllabic terminology which, they say, is not just vague but pompously empty. In short, there is no general consensus that "equilibration" is among the highest of Piaget's achievements: many psychologists asked to rank his contributions would award equilibration not the first prize, not even the consolation prize, but the booby prize.

Those who require precision above all else will have learnt long since not to seek it *chez* Piaget. But vague ideas can serve the heuristic purpose of keeping important questions alive, if empirically dormant, when better concepts do not yet exist for dealing with them. They may engender a family of speculations some or all of which can eventually be given specific empirical content— "eventually", because it may not be immediately apparent how one might map a given speculative vocabulary onto observable phenomena. One may have to await future conceptual and/or empirical advances in whose terms the initial speculations can be interpreted. If an idea is intended as a substantive unifying concept applicable to distinct theoretical domains, then parallel empirical specifications should eventually be possible in each field. For instance, the abstract concept of cybernetic "feedback" (which Piaget saw as very close to that of equilibration) can be applied with varying degrees of rigour to many different phenomena, from warm-bloodedness to the political process.

These considerations spawn seven questions: (1) Did Piaget identify a question of theoretical significance which is worth keeping alive in vague terms until better ones become available? (2) Does "equilibration" offer anything over and above more familiar concepts, such as "feedback"? (3) Did he provide the specifications necessary for his concept's fruitful application in all or any of the relevant disciplines? (4) Are there other, more recent, ideas (specifically: computational ones) which address the same range of questions more satisfactorily? (5) If so, are these ideas so consonant with his approach that they may be seen as filling out his own account of equilibration, or are they totally unrelated to his work? (6) Can his concept of equilibration, interpreted in computational terms, identify radical development not only in infancy but also in adult life? (7) Last, can there be (as Piaget claimed) a truly general theory of equilibration? The subsequent sections address these questions in turn.

The Underlying Problem

The prime theoretical problem addressed by Piaget in terms of equilibration is the development of harmonious novelties. In embryogenesis and histogenesis, for example, genuinely new structures are somehow created out of older ones, without any functional impairment of the working of the system as a whole. This sort of creativity, where structures arise *de novo*, differs from that wherein (possibly unique) phenomena are generated which are different from but of the same essential form as those existing previously, and of which an example is the sort of creativity attributed by Chomsky to language. It differs even more from the effecting of chaotic changes, that is, of changes which may arise in a principled fashion (in that they are caused rather than random events), but which have no tendency to cohere with the overall organization of the system as a whole and so often lead to malfunction—of which the obvious example is genetic mutation. In general, when new structures are differentiated out of more primitive ones, we need to explain how overall integration can be maintained as the system develops from its more primitive to its more complex form.

As Piaget put it, speaking of both mental and physical life, we need to understand "how the mechanism bringing about this continual construction may constitute at the same time a regulating mechanism ensuring coherence. In the field of the cognitive functions in particular, the problem is to understand how learning, discovery and creation may not only be reconciled with but take place at the same time as control and verification in such a way that the new remains in harmony with the acquired" [Piaget, 1958, p. 832]. Other psychological (and biological) theorists, he said, discussed some of the novelties created but typically ignored the problem of how their creation could be harmoniously integrated. He claimed that his account of equilibration provided a solution to this problem.

Equally, he claimed thereby to have exhibited the continuity, or essential similarity, of cognitive and biological development. He even said that the "true perspective" of the equilibrium factor "is a biological and not a logical one, although the special equilibrium of logical structures is one of the finest achievements of living morphogenesis" [Piaget, 1958, p. 837]. The term "equilibrium" (like "assimilation" and "accommodation" too) originated in a biological context, wherein it refers to the maintenance of the internal environment. But Piaget saw embryological *homeorhesis* as even more like cognitive growth than is physiological *homeostasis*. That is, he saw the development of cognitive schemata and the morphogenesis of the embryo as two special cases of the same phenomenon, namely, the (largely autonomous) continuing increase of differentiation within a system whose overall integration is retained throughout.

Equilibration and Feedback

As regards "equilibration" and "feedback", Piaget spoke of the former before Wiener identified the latter. So insofar as the two concepts are equivalent, this is a case of a later concept's clarifying an earlier, less well-defined, one. However, there is a significant difference between them. In classic examples of feedback, whether in biological homeostasis or control engineering, the central problem is how to arrive at and maintain a steady state by varying parameters whose potential relevance is already given. Even when the feedback controls a non-steady state (as in the braking of a large vehicle), the relevant constraints are explicitly allowed for in the design of the system. But Piaget's interest was in more complex cases, in which integrative control has to be maintained throughout a continuing process of structural differentiation. In differentiation, new parameters arise in respect of which to solve—and to posit—problems of system-maintenance. Thus once liver and lungs appear, certain problems of overall control can be solved in ways not previously available to the organism; but, by the same token, new problems are posited concerning the mutual regulation of these organs themselves. Accordingly, different theoretical problems arise with regard to homeostasis and to homeorhesis. Insofar as Piaget's "equilibration" stresses the latter rather than the former it is not simply equivalent to "feedback". Indeed, as I have argued elsewhere [Boden, 1979, ch. 7], the concept of feedback (like algebraic concepts also) is inadequate to express complex structural changes of the sort that take place in cognitive and morphogenetic development.

The vagueness of "equilibration"

Piaget was right to identify autonomous differentiation as a very important, very general, and profoundly problematic phenomenon. There are great difficulties in conceptualizing coherent, progressive, self-regulated change, whether it occurs within cognitive structures, biological organisms, social systems, or scientific knowledge. For instance, despite their many disagreements, Popper and Kuhn agree that scientific revolutions are not the result of any rationally reconstructable process of discovery. If they are right, their failure to conceptualize science as a harmonious self-generative process is of course no failure; but if they are wrong, we still await such a conceptualization (for an attempt to discover structural continuities in so-called scientific "revolutions", see [Krige, 1980]). Within sociology, the difficulty of conceptualizing non-revolutionary social change is notorious. The orderly creation of new and functionally integrated forms in embryogenesis is acknowledged as an unsolved problem of theoretical biology, and some biologists (like Piaget) regard the origin of new genera and species in evolution as inexplicable by neo-Darwinism. And the development of cognitive structures, the increasing differentiation yet overall integration of knowledge and inferential power, is likewise obscure.

This last comment may seem strange, for Piaget devoted a lifetime's work to this very issue. Certainly, his discussions of cognitive change were more useful than his remarks on biological development. He suggested hidden complexities in the development of cognitive structures, and drew attention to many interesting empirical phenomena. But he did not clarify the equilibratory aspects of development, because he failed to specify the concept of equilibration to any useful degree. His remarks about equilibration, suggestive though some of them may be, are of such extreme generality and abstractness as not to be even *prima facie* applicable to clearly distinct empirical phenomena.

For instance, he taught that equilibrium is a matter of degree: according to Piaget, all living structures are equilibrated, but some are more equilibrated than others. He claimed that complete equilibrium is reached with the (fully reversible) formal operations, whose structures and transformations he defined in terms of algebraic lattices. Prior to this stage, he said, "equilibrium is only a compromise at the level of organic morphogenesis or variation of the species. With nervous organization and mental life . . . a twofold power of retroaction and anticipation considerably enlarges the field of this equilibrium and replaces fleeting compromises by actual syntheses" [Piaget, 1958, p. 837]. Again, he claimed to have distinguished three types of equilibration: between the subject's mental schemata and external objects; between the subschemes within a given overall scheme, some of which may have started life as independent schemes; and between the (hierarchically distinct) parts of knowledge and the totality of knowledge. About the latter, he said: "Little by little there has to be a constant equilibrium established between the parts of the subject's knowledge and the totality of his knowledge at any given moment. There is a constant differentiation of the totality of knowledge into the parts and an integration of the parts back into the whole" [Piaget, 1975, p. 839]. He insisted that in all cases of equilibration, "the activities of the subject are always compensatory as well as constructive," and in a similar spirit spoke of "the functional necessity of negations," saying that equilibrium can involve processing as many negations as affirmations, implicit though these negations may be [Piaget, 1977, p. 11]. And he often spoke of cognitive equilibration as being "fed" by input from the outside world, as needing "nourishment" much as organisms do.

None of these remarks is at all clear. Just *what* are the compensations, regulations, or negations involved in any particular case? And just *how* do they contribute to the overall control of cognitive function? Piaget's writing was not sufficiently precise to answer these questions, or even to state them adequately. In his lengthy discussion of what he called the "how" of equilibration [Piaget, 1977], he struggled manfully with the vocabulary of "positive" and "negative disturbances", "regulations", and "regulations of regulations". Disturbances are what trigger equilibration, being "gaps that leave some requirement unfulfilled," gaps to be defined in terms of currently functioning cognitive schemata. Regulations are the adjustments made in response to disturbances, including disturbances that arise because of previous regulations. In describing the self-correcting action of a bicycle-rider, for example, Piaget said "As for outside obstacles, these are avoided, which means compensating for the disturbances by a whole or partial negation, the latter corresponding to a differentiation of the scheme into subschemes which determine whether or not the goal can be attained by a direct itinerary" [Piaget, 1977, p. 26]. But this is merely a roundabout way of saying that there are complex processes of problem-solving going on, without specifying them or even clearly articulating the general sorts of complexity that might be involved.

However, if Piaget's own account of the mechanisms of equilibration does not do the job he set out to do, perhaps some other version of his theory might. This raises the fourth and fifth questions listed above: Are there any recent concepts that can express the same phenomena more adequately, and if so are these wholly unrelated to Piaget's ideas or can his talk of equilibration fruitfully be interpreted in terms of them? The next section discusses these questions together, while the last applies them not only to infancy but to cognitive development in adult life (that is, to creativity).

Computational concepts in relation to Piaget's ideas

Concepts drawn from computer science and artificial intelligence are especially promising here [Boden, 1987; 1979]. These ideas owe nothing in their provenance to Piaget, but it does not follow that Piaget's work cannot reasonably be interpreted in their terms. However, we must be careful not to cheat here, not to speak of "interpretation" where we should rather speak of "substitution". We must not put words into the mouth of a reconstructed Piaget, which the unreconstructed Piaget would not have been prepared to accept. Even where there is some degree of conceptual affinity, so that straightforward *substitution* is not at issue, we must remember that it is one thing to say that he said something, another to say that he would (or might) have said it if he had been given the chance, and yet another to say that he could have said it without falling into incoherence.

I have argued elsewhere that Piaget's commitment to cybernetics, his formalism, his structuralism, and his semiotic mentalism all predisposed him to sympathy (which he occasionally expressed) for a computational approach to theoretical psychology [Boden, 1979, ch. 7]. Similarly, I have argued that his vision of a cognitive biology is essentially consonant with recent developments in theoretical morphology, which are themselves influenced by computational ideas [Boden, 1979, ch. 6; Boden, 1981b]. So although Piaget did not use computational concepts, relying instead on algebraic and cybernetic formalizations (which as I said above are incapable of expressing a rich variety of structures and transformational processes), he probably would not have been averse to a computational interpretation of his work. Taking this as a license, then, how might one use current computational ideas to clarify and elaborate his views on equilibration, views expressed in remarks like those quoted above?

Piaget described organizations in terms of "part" and "whole", but these concepts are problematic for computational systems involving recursion—such as many programs, and the human mind [Hofstadter, 1979]. In recursive systems, a procedure functioning on a problem of one level can activate itself to solve a similar problem on a lower level. Likewise, procedure A can call on procedure B to solve a problem, and while B is dealing with this problem it can call on A to resolve a difficulty of its own. Is B part of A, or A part of B? Even within a single program, no sensible general answer can be given. However, if the particular processing-point and problem concerned are specified, one can distinguish between B's functioning under the control of A and A's being subordinated to B (one can specify the "regulations of regulations" involved).

Piaget also erred in having an overly static view of organization. Despite his many reminders that the mind is a dynamic system, he represented it in essentially non-dynamic terms. For example, he relied on algebraic lattices to express properties of transformational systems, such as reversibility. This is not surprising, since computational concepts did not then exist with which to describe types of transformations and the relations between them. Such concepts are likely to be helpful here because they are expressly designed to represent dynamic processes and the organization of control within functioning systems.

Partly due to his lack of dynamic concepts, Piaget's notion of organization was simplistically hierarchical, and his understanding of integration limited accordingly. Much as biologists distinguish organism, organ-system, organ, cell, and organelle, so Piaget conceptualized cognitive hierarchies as systems wherein every member exists on a specific level, being clearly subordinate or superordinate to its neighbours. Computational work has given us a richer (though undoubtedly still primitive) sense of what sorts of organization there may be.

For example, hierarchy, in which control always passes either up or down between adjacent levels and has to follow fixed pathways, has been contrasted with heterarchy, in which control is much more flexible according to context [Winston, 1972]. Hierarchy is likened to a rigid bureaucracy, while heterarchy resembles a committee of experts, each doing their own thing in their own way except when they recognize the need for help on a specific difficulty from some other expert. "Production systems", too, have an organization very different from a hierarchy. These are sets of functionally independent rules, each of which performs a specific action when a particular condition pertains. The system is developed by the successive addition of independent rules. Yet the "regulations" performed by such a system may be surprisingly coherent and intelligent overall—indeed, Piagetian "seriation" has been modelled in these terms [Young, 1976]. Admittedly, as soon as a production system becomes really complex, additional organization has to be somehow introduced, which goes against the spirit of the initial philosophy [Davis & King, 1977]. But although it is still unclear how different types of organization compare in their ability to carry out computations (equilibratory regulations) of various sorts, the sorts of questions that need to be asked about such matters are becoming clearer.

This is relevant to Piaget's notion of equilibrated coordination between subschemes. If two systems are to function in concert, information received by one (whether resulting from external events or from its own physical or computational actions) has to be made available to the other if it is likely to be relevant to its functioning. For instance, if grasping and looking are to be coordinated (and irrespective of whether some degree of coordination is present from birth, or whether they begin their development independently), then proprioceptive and visual information have to reach the cross-modal scheme in a coordinated fashion. One way in which information can pass from one system to another is by direct communication between them; another is *via* a central memory-store, or "blackboard", allowing messages to be written and read by both subsystems. These sorts of computationally distinct equilibratory regulation do not exhaust the possibilities (for instance, there could be a number of largely independent "blackboards"—or memories—each communicating with a subset of the system's functions). And neither of them as just described explains how the need for or appropriateness of certain information is recognized by a system, on its own or on another's behalf. If a computer program is to function then these questions must be given provisional answers, but our ignorance about the specifics of coordination in the human case is still enormous.

We are even ignorant about the general question of how much coordination exists within the mind. Piaget's remarks often imply that adult human knowledge is a seamless robe, enjoying a degree of integration that allows of no inherent contradictions and provides for coordinate relations between every part. This seems to be implicit in his claim that "little by little there has to be a constant equilibrium established between the parts of the subject's knowledge and the totality of his knowledge at any given moment." This vision of knowledge is also commonly the epistemologist's ideal (which partly accounts for Piaget's own commitment to it). But work in artificial intelligence has suggested that knowledge may be modular, with limited opportunities of coordination between the various modules, and that potential contradictions can exist within a knowledge-system without prejudicing its functioning. Considerations of computational efficiency show that both these features can afford positive advantages to a knowledge-system, so they are of epistemological as well as psychological importance. Again, the dynamics of the system are crucial: whereas an actual contradiction (such as "All birds can fly, but some can't") is no use to anybody, a potential contradiction (such as that between "All birds can fly" and "Emus are birds that can't fly") may cause no problem, provided that when remarks about emus are accessed or generated the system is somehow protected from being led into practical difficulties by the (false) over-generalization about birds present elsewhere within it.

To ask "how much" coordination there is in the mind, as I did above, is itself problematic, for it implies that coordination can be measured. Certainly, gross comparative judgments can be made of the relative degree of coordination of different systems. This is done by the computer scientist in assessing the extent of communication between component modules of a system, by the psychiatrist in diagnosing "dissociated" personality or consciousness, and of course by Piaget in speaking of more and less complete stages of equilibration. But we saw above that communication can be direct or indirect, which suggests that measurement of coordination is not a straightforward matter. Again, potential coordination has to be distinguished from actual (or normal) coordination. The development of a measure of coordination, or integration, is a matter for abstract computational logic, closely linked to the measurement of system-complexity. But it seems most implausible that any useful notion of "complete" coordination will be formulated, broadly equivalent to Piaget's "complete" equilibrium.

If Piaget's talk of "nourishment" is more than just a way of saying that minds (like organisms) are open systems affected by the environment, it is perhaps comparable to a remark made in computational circles, that "the cheapest store of information about the real world is the real world." This remark reflects the difficulty of providing programs with enough data and inferential power to compute the properties of the external world. Comparably, evolution apparently has not managed to produce cognitive systems that can function flexibly in the real world without taking in information from it. Even animals with a preprogrammed ability to behave in a given way usually rely on real-world input (the "innate releasing stimulus") to tell them when to do so. On this view, that equilibration should be dialectical is a computational necessity.

It might be objected that all these computational reinterpretations of Piaget are irrelevant to the most interesting feature of his concept of equilibration. No-one familiar with computational models, or even with Chomsky's grammar, would deny that finite sets of generative rules can give rise to historically novel phenomena sharing a certain structure. Insofar as this is what Piaget was claiming in speaking of the creation of harmonious novelties, he was clearly right, although he did not specify any generative rules himself. But Piaget also emphasized systems where the structuring principles themselves change over time in an integrated fashion. A computationalist interpretation and/or critique of Piaget's work must address this type of "equilibration" too.

Equilibration and Creativity

Piaget's emphasis on "accommodation" implied that all structural change is based on the commission, recognition, and correction of failures. But children drawing maps, for example, spontaneously improve their spatial representations even without the spur of failure [Karmiloff-Smith, 1979]. Their increased computational efficiency enables them to solve problems later that they could not have solved before, but it was not forced on them by any earlier mistake. In general, it is not clear that differentiation is motored by incapacity (the foetus is a viable organism, and the ammonite is a viable species). Accordingly, an adequate theoretical account of differentiation would presumably have to identify some autonomous tendency to (or, at least, potential for) self-improvement, irrespective of any response to the pressures of failure. While Piaget posited such a tendency, and even regarded the rise of logic and mathematics as an evolutionary inevitability, it cannot be said that he gave us any clear idea of how it might function.

The essential reason for the inadequacy of theories of cognitive change focussed on failure is their implicit assumption that organisms always aim at some specific goal. For a failure involves an inability to do something specific, in that the concept "failure" invites the question "failure to do *what?*" In fact, creatures do not always aim at pre-defined goals, but often appear to delight in activity for its own sake. Or rather, as Piaget himself at times pointed out, they commonly aim at goals (such as economy, clarity, elegance, and interestingness) which are high-level meta-goals that control the adaptive exploration of their own cognitive processes. Because people commonly think of "goal-directedness" in terms of relatively specific, well-defined goals, to conceive of equilibration in terms of response to failure is to risk losing sight of the exploratory aspects of thought and action. Learning and development—and creativity likewise—are not mere responses to failure, which is neither necessary nor sufficient for adaptation. They are controlled by more general considerations than match-mismatch with a specific goal-state, and they are grounded in some relatively autonomous creative urge.

How can we conceptualize this equilibratory urge (the evolutionary advantage of which is obvious)? And can we do so in a way which illuminates the nature of "creativity" in childhood or adult life? Like the "track and trail strategies of lowly organisms" [Selfridge, in press], it must both lead the creature to engage spontaneously in novel behaviour, and enable it to take advantage of the results when this exploration throws up something useful. This of course implies that the creature has available some form of evaluation function in terms of which it can recognize something "useful", or at least "interesting". If creative exploration is not to degenerate (*sic*) into mere chaotic novelty, the generation of new forms, as well as their consequent evaluation, must take place within certain structural constraints. In general, to understand an example of equilibration, or creativity, would be to have a theory of the various transformations, at more or less basic levels, by which the relevant structural potential can be selectively explored.

For instance, mathematical, scientific, and artistic creativity involve the deliberate exploration and disciplined transformation, or relaxation, of structural constraints. Non-Euclidean geometry originated in the (deliberate) dropping of Euclid's last axiom. Kekule's discovery of the benzene ring involved the (unconscious) transformation of one topological structure into another: it is significant that Kekule dreamt not of a little girl's hoop, but of a snake biting its tail—in other words, of a closed curve that one would have expected to be an open curve. A prime root of Einstein's creative achievement was his query whether the concept of simultaneity can be analysed and the resultant "parts" variously combined to form distinct conceptual structures. And the development of tonal into atonal music, in broadly the way in which this happened, can with hindsight be seen as intelligible, and even inevitable [Rosen, 1978]. In all of these cases, of course, the initial transformation (which may or may not have been consciously effected) was followed by some sort of evaluative assessment, whether by mathematical proof, experimental method, or artistic discipline. Everyday adaptation presumably involves similar transformational processes, with varying opportunities for conscious initiation and/or control, and varying criteria of "interestingness".

In the biological domain, a theory of morphological creativity would explain how it is possible for a gill-slit to be transformed into a thyroid gland, or a normal blastula into a deformed embryo or non-viable monster; also, it would explain why certain fabulous beasts could only have been imagined, not created [Boden, 1981b]. In biology as in psychology, we need some account of processes that can explore the space defined by background creative constraints, and of processes that can transform these constraints themselves.

Although some psychologists have stressed the role of exploratory play in the development of cognitive skills, positing autonomous motives such as "competence" or "curiosity", they have said little or nothing about mental structures [White, 1959]. Piaget, by contrast, realized the need for some concept of autonomous adaptation characterized in structural terms. His account of equilibration sought to illuminate the way in which new, more differentiated, structures arise "spontaneously" out of simpler ones, whether in cultural, psychological, embryological, or evolutionary development. But to seek is not necessarily to find: the vagueness of Piaget's concept of equilibration has been remarked *ad nauseam* .

The general comments (about recursion, hierarchy, and intermodular communication) in the previous section indicated how a computational approach might identify such vaguenesses, and improve upon them. Can anything helpful be said in computational terms about the underlying mechanisms of creativity, which might support Piaget's suggestion of a deep affinity between the historical development of theoretical ideas in science and the development of cognitive structures in the infant mind?

Current "self-adaptive" programs are mostly concerned with the fine tuning of already structurally adapted computational systems, rather than with their structural adaptation itself. Some of them, too, overemphasize the role of failure [*e.g.* Winston, 1975], although others [*e.g.* Samuel, 1970] use a hill-climbing strategy controlled by some notion of "getting better". Almost nothing has been done to model systems where the structuring principles themselves change over time in an integrated fashion. This is a key notion in understanding development and creativity, and this was what primarily concerned Piaget.

For example, Winston's program can recognize only a few properties of the input, these being all and only the relevant ones, each of which was initially defined by the programmer [Winston, 1975]. Given these predefined properties, the program can learn from counterexamples as well as from examples, but only if they are presented to it in an epistemologically suitable (highly constrained) order. Living organisms are not so limited. Moreover, in real life, features which once were irrelevant may later become useful spurs to further improvement. For instance, studies of "consolidation" in children's understanding of balance-problems suggests that features are initially ignored as (Kuhnian?) anomalies which later come to be regarded as counterexamples enabling refinement of the child's current theory [Inhelder & Karmiloff-Smith, 1975]. The computational basis of these changes is obscure: how is an exception (a "disturbance") recognized as such, how is it classified as anomaly or as counterexample, and how is it used to guide development of the system?

Analogous questions are addressed in some degree by another learning program, closer in spirit to Piaget's views on cognitive development. It uses meta-commentary and self-criticism to improve on its past performance, and generalizes its fresh insights so that they can be applied to many new problems of the same structural form [Sussman, 1975]. Unlike the previous example, this program can perhaps be seen as relevant to differentiation, for the internal structure of its self-generated plans becomes increasingly complex, and it produces computational routines specifically designed to effect the coordination of newly generated subsystems. For instance, it not only generates distinct plans for achieving different subgoals, but it discovers that an extra step sometimes has to be inserted between the completion of one and the start of another (like taking the old cotton out of one's needle before trying to thread it with the new). However, this program learns only by reflecting on its failures (which it classifies into five types according to structural principles). Admittedly, the structure of its problem-solving does become more complex and differentiated, and better adapted to the specific constraints of the problem-situation. Its creative potential is however very limited, for it is capable of exploring only a small number of transformational paths.

Humans can try out many new ways of thinking to see what they will find. They need not have any problem in mind, to which they hope the exploration may be relevant; even if they do, they may be very unclear about how this could be so. Admittedly, where a newly acquired structure is concerned, people often explore its generative potential *without* making any attempt to transform the structure itself. For instance, children practise grammatical permutations of words when left alone in their cribs [Weir, 1962]. And, as we have seen, children sometimes ignore a failure as an irrelevant anomaly instead of treating it (as Piagetian theory would predict) as a spur to adaptation. The experimenters suggested that they need time for "consolidation" of their new theories—but what is consolidation, and why is it necessary?

One common example of consolidation was apparently recognized by Descartes, whose fourth rule of reason was: "Recapitulate!". This advice is not so banal as it may seem, for recapitulation of an argument (for example, going over and over a geometrical proof) may lead one to "see directly" relations which earlier one could only infer by remembering a series of steps. (In Descartes' terms *deduction* gives way to *intuition*.) And rereading a proof, paper, or program enables one not only to eliminate mistakes, but to find economies, generalizations, and improvements in clarity. Recapitulation, that is, seems to be one method of achieving a measure of consolidation.

To ask how recapitulation leads to consolidation, and how consolidation is achieved by other types of thinking, is to ask how cognitive structures can be transformed, compared, and amended by exploratory processes primarily concerned with the inner world, as opposed to the outer environment. To speak of equilibrations here is to speak of internal equilibrations: mutual accommodations and assimilations of mental structures decoupled from the outside world, and informing the mind at relatively deep levels. Computational ideas are useful in this context because they suggest some specific types of equilibratory process that might be involved.

In general, during the period of consolidation one does things that enable one to represent and improve the structure of the cognitive structure itself. That is, one engages in meta-activities, and/or one follows high-level meta-goals, of various kinds [cf. Rissland, 1978]. So one eliminates redundant steps; one constructs higher-level representations that economically summarize a number of already available sub-structures; one explores the sorts of transformation allowed by the unfamiliar structure; one classifies the states that can be generated within it; and one compares this structure with others in various ways. (The first two of these mental activities are involved also in *planning* , a feature of economical problem-solving that has been widely studied in computational terms [Boden, 1987, ch. 12].)

Until one thus understands the general potential of structure, one may not be motivated to change it, nor able fruitfully to pay attention to counterexamples to it. T. S. Kuhn's [1962] account of the activity of normal science, which continues despited theoretical anomalies, seems to fit this description. So does the exploration of any new artistic style before it is superceded by another. Once consolidation has been achieved, other meta-processes may come into play (*sic*) by which relatively radical changes can be effected. For example, dropping a very basic constraint (such as Euclid's last axiom, or the "string-like" nature of molecules) may lead to a coherent structure with generative properties very different from its predecessor. Again, combining sub-structures or procedures in different combinations, and with different orders of priority, may be a general method by which the mind can spontaneously generate new structures out of old. The technique of "brainstorming" is based on this principle.

If consolidation is a mapping of the generative geography of one's current structures, a theory of creative equilibration should explain how one realizes that the terrain has now been reasonably well-mapped, so that more adventurous explorations may be appropriate. Clearly, one's judgments about the extent of unexplored territory must influence the evaluation of what is "interesting". This self-tuning (whereby what is of interest today may be boring tomorrow) is analogous to the successive strengthening of evaluation criteria in "track and trail" adaptation. But in the human case the criterion is non-metric and multidimensional: one may have explored some aspects of a structure to one's satisfaction—indeed, satiation—but not others.

An adaptive system must also be able to judge the "interest" of the results of its (more or less radical) explorations, and of the exploratory paths it decides to follow. Without this control, which determines what the exploring mind will find worth pursuing, exploration would degrade into mere chaotic thrashing about. Literary criticism, criticism of music or the visual arts, critical history of ideas, and scientific discussion all aim to express our intuitions in this regard. A psychological theory of creativity should try to make these insights even more explicit. This problem is not seriously addressed by the theories of "adaptation-levels", "discrepancy principles", and the like [e.g. Helson, 1959], which equate degree of interest with degree of novelty (novelty being measured with respect to the subject's current schemas, or competence). Adaptation is not a matter of nobbling the new, but of pursuing the promising.

A study of creativity which has addressed this question is D. B. Lenat's automatic mathematician [Lenat, 1977]. This program uses several hundred heuristics (not just a few transformational rules) to explore the space defined by a hundred primitive concepts. "Exploration" here means asking about certain facets of a given (primitive or constructed) concept. For instance: is it named; is it a generalization or a special case of some other concept; what examples fit the definition of the concept; which operations can operate on it, and which can result in it; are there any similar concepts; and what are some potential theorems involving the concept? One of the facets is "interestingness": Lenat attempts to control the exploration by guiding it into areas likely to be more adaptive than others. For instance, he provides it with the general heuristic that if the union of two sets has a simply expressible property not possessed by either of them, then it is probably worth exploring. Lenat claims to have identified several very general heuristics, but also stresses the need for large numbers of domain-specific, knowledge-based, heuristics (some of which are specializations of the more general ones).

Granted that the heuristics were thought up by Lenat rather than by the program, it is significant (and surprising to many people) that this sort of fruitful exploratory thinking can be formally represented at all. However, the degree of creativity evinced by the program is difficult to assess. Critics [Ritchie & Hanna, 1984] have remarked that Lenat does not list all the concepts regarded by the program as interesting: perhaps a high proportion were mathematically trivial. It is not clear from the published accounts whether some crucial "discoveries" were made possible only by the use of unacceptably *ad hoc* heuristics, nor is it easy to draw the line between an acceptably specialized expert heuristic and a disingenuous programming trick. Certainly, many of the heuristics are highly domain-specific, relevant only to set-theory.

Perhaps similar considerations concerning creative exploration might illuminate various biological phenomena which, on a neo-Darwinist account of evolution, are very puzzling. These include the facts that the fraction of DNA that does not code for the synthesis of specific proteins increases phylogenetically; that species have evolved remarkably quickly, and that the more complex species have if anything evolved at a greater rate than their predecessors; and that the speed at which a species evolves morphologically seems quite unrelated to the rate at which its individual proteins evolve (so frogs have protein-synthesizing mechanisms of comparable complexity to those of man). Such facts are not explicable in terms of "Random-Generate-and-Test", the mutational strategy favoured by neo-Darwinism. This is because (as was discovered by the early workers in automatic programming), the combinatorics of such a process are horrendous [cf. Arbib, 1969]. Switching to a higher-level biological language (*cf.* "consolidation"), might be effected by random processes of gene duplication and recombination; but this merely reduces the exponent without preventing an exponential explosion.

Instead, some strategy of "Plausible-Generate-and-Test" is needed, whereby mutations of a type likely to be adaptive become increasingly probable. The initial heuristics must evolve by random mutation (since there is no suggestion of teleology here), but these survive by natural selection and can eventually enable a form of biological bootstrapping by modifying each other. This is possible because they are embodied as DNA and their "target" for interpretation is itself DNA. That is, they are heuristics recommending certain "copying errors" and preventing others. The sort of transformational processes they influence are gene substitution, insertion, deletion, translocation, inversion, recombination, segregation, and transposition.

In a speculative paper [Lenat, 1980], Lenat likens these transformational processes to Production Rules, saying the IF... part of the heuristic might be specified by proximity on the DNA molecule, whereas the THEN... part could direct gene rearrangement, duplication, placement of the mutators and intervening sequences, and so on. For instance, one heuristic might be that gene recombinations should involve neighbour-genes rather than genes at opposite ends of the DNA string: in a creature where genes for morphologically related structures happened to lie next to each other, this heuristic would encourage mutations of both genes together, which would tend toward a structurally integrated evolution.

Even if we had a useful theory of creative heuristics, we could not use it to predict the creative phenomena of the future: new ideas or new species would still surprise us. For a theory of creative heuristics, or of the cognitive explorations indicated above, would be a theory of competence rather than performance. Piaget's theory of equilibration, likewise, is a competence-theory. Its aim is not to predict just what a particular child will do at a certain time, but to identify what classes of behaviour can or cannot occur and to explain their possibility in terms of generative structures within the mind.

The unpredictability of those mental phenomena we call creative is due partly to the fact that the mind's generative potential is infinite. Our concepts, cognitive structures, and transformational heuristics are so diverse, so many-levelled, so idiosyncratic, and so richly associated that their cumulative generative potential can only be glimpsed, not grasped.

The second reason for the unpredictability of creative thoughts is the contingency which surrounds us: the complexity of the outside world, and the fact that it goes its own way independently of our designs. We cannot hope to predict the uncovered agar-plate left on Fleming's window-sill, nor even his creative response to it. But a theory of creative competence could help us to understand how Fleming's consequent discovery of penicillin was possible. A structural-transformational theory of equilibration need not deny a creative role to contingencies, provided that they can be integrated into the mental structure concerned by way of the criteria of interestingness already functioning within the mind. Serendipity is no accident.

Equilibration as a General Process

Piaget assumed that there can be a general theory of equilibration. Many computationally inclined psychologists share his faith, at least as regards cognitive phenomena. And some workers in artificial intelligence are seeking a theory applicable alike to machines, Martians, monkeys, and men.

However, other such workers have abandoned their hopes that very general principles of reasoning might be found in terms of which to articulate all intelligent processes. Thus Lenat's insistence that creativity in exploring set-theory depends on already knowing which heuristics are likely to be mathematically relevant is grounded in his belief (shared with many AI-researchers) that intelligence depends heavily on expert knowledge as opposed to general skills. Many cases of intelligence seem to rely on large amounts of task-specific knowledge, which are sometimes specifically allowed for in the hardware (like early visual processing in the retina [Marr, 1976; 1982]), and sometimes have to be learnt.

If Fleming had not already known a great deal about bacteriology, and about what healthy bacterial colonies—and errant moulds—look like on agar-plates, he would never have generated his hunch that the green spots on the unprotected agar-jelly were bactericidal. Whether we are concerned with antibiotics, seriation, set-theory, or genetic evolution, to explain creative development we need to posit specialist as well as general heuristics. Naturally, some general concepts have a widespread relevance; for instance: recursion, methods of communication between one module or task and another, or the distinction between depth-first and breadth-first search. Likewise, natural selection is a very general way of assessing biological "interest" *post hoc*. But adaptation requires one—whether infant, adult, or species—to learn a large number of special tricks in terms of which to generate things likely to be interesting, and many special principles with which to evaluate the interest of anything that turns up.

Insofar as this is so, the extent to which one can hope for a *general* theory of equilibration, or of creativity, is limited. However, such heuristic tricks and principles function against a background of creative constraints, in whose terms structural equilibration in various domains is basically intelligible. So while Piaget's faith in the possibility of a general theory of cognitive equilibration is not obviously mistaken, it is not obviously correct either. Still less is it obvious (though I have claimed that it is possible) that general principles of equilibration may be involved in all forms of development, whether cognitive, biological, or social.

Conclusion

Despite its vagueness, and the unclarity of its research implications, Piaget's theory of equilibration merits attention. It identifies an important theoretical problem—how the generation of harmonious novelties is possible—which is still highly obscure, despite some relevant scientific advances. These are situated within developmental biology, cybernetics, and artificial intelligence or computational psychology. The computational approach supports Piaget's claim that there are very general questions here, whose solution in different domains—although differing greatly in detail—may in very abstract terms be significantly similar.

Piaget was mistaken in thinking that as well as indicating the problem he had provided its solution. Understandably, many critics regard it as wellnigh devilish on his part to have tempted his disciples into the illusory faith that "equilibration" provides an *explanation*. But to point out significant problems that are largely unrecognized by other theorists is no mean feat. Even the devil must be given his due.

Chapter 8

Artificial Intelligence and Biological Intelligence

I. *Introduction*

It is often said that there can be no such thing as artificial intelligence. For certain, there is no such thing as biological intelligence. There are, however, biological *intelligences*. Animals have evolved many different motor and perceptual strategies to cope with the world—indeed, these strategies are so different that one might rather say "their worlds", as we shall see. The "space" of biological intelligences is not yet fully charted, nor have all the relevant dimensions been identified. I shall argue that this exploration and theoretical mapping may benefit from some of the insights of artificial intelligence (AI).

Biologists often doubt that AI could possibly throw light on animal intelligence. For computers are very unlike brains. They are made of quite different stuff, and most are digital, serial-processing (and general-purpose) devices. Furthermore, AI-workers typically ignore neuroscience. The intellectual divide seems deep: how can AI be of interest to biologists?

The accusation that AI ignores biology is broadly correct. But, as we shall see, ideas from neuroscience are playing a larger role in AI now than in the past. During the 1960's and 1970's, research in AI-vision (for example) had abandoned the early attempts of the 1950's to mimic the parallel embodiment of the brain. Instead, it focused on discovering the knowledge (and the ways of using it) involved in vision, on the computational functions required for the basic task of sight: 2D-to-3D mapping. (Comparable work was being done in other areas of AI, with respect to the computational constraints on different information-processing tasks.) It was because the computational functions necessary for sight had not yet been properly identified that the early parallel-processing models of vision had to be abandoned. Recently, however, some of the special features of brains—their parallelism and dedicated machinery—are being taken seriously again in AI-vision (and in the modeling of language and memory too).

Even those computer-modelers who work with parallel ("connectionist") systems still live in happy ignorance of biochemistry. For those properties of brains which enable them to function as organs of intelligence almost certainly have less to do with what they are made of, than with how they are organized and —above all—what it is that they do. AI-workers concentrate on the latter two questions: on the identification, in abstract terms, of specific computational functions, and on the way in which computational units can be organized so as to carry out those functions.

This process may cast light on how we, and other animals, do things. For at least some of the computational processes in computers (whether parallel or not) may be significantly similar to the processes going on in human brains. So psychology and ethology can expect to profit from AI. (And AI can profit from psychology and ethology, which provide a rich source of examples drawn from the space of intelligent phenomena.)

Even neuroscience, the study of "wetware", might profit from AI—indeed, it already has. It was the abstract computational arguments about perception put forward in the late 1950's by the programmer of *Pandemonium* (an early computer model of vision) which first suggested that feature-detectors might exist in the nervous system [Selfridge, 1959], and which prompted neurophysiologists to search for them (initially, in the frog's retina [Lettvin, Maturana, Pitts, & McCulloch, 1959]). Computer scientists can tell neuroscientists nothing about the material nature of the brain. But they may (as in this case) be able to suggest what sort of *functional* unit neuroscientists might fruitfully look for. Correlatively, neuroscience may suggest that certain sorts of organization can be put to good computational effect in generating intelligent behaviour.

I shall argue that an explanation of biological intelligence must credit many animals besides man with the ability to form representations—and the concepts of AI are specifically concerned with representations, and their transformations. "Representation" is not a concept of physiology (the term "cerebral model" is a psycho-physiological hybrid), so the physiological differences between brains and computers do not make AI biologically irrelevant. The foundations of an adequate explanation of "intelligence" would consist of abstract analyses of the information-processing tasks carried out by various species. Resting on these foundations would be an account of the computational processes that perform those tasks, and (ideally) of how they are embodied in the neurophysiology of organisms.

Like the ancient city of Romulus and Remus, this explanatory edifice will not be built in a day. We shall see that the problems of formulating plausible hypotheses about representations in animal (and human) minds are even more complex than is generally believed. The moral of this paper, then, is not that AI-workers have achieved solutions to ethologists' problems, but that AI raises theoretical questions about intelligence which ethologists should not ignore.

In Section II, I say something in general terms about AI as the study of representation, and explain why it suggests that we must attribute representations even to non-communicating animals. Next, I relate some problems about motor action (Section III) and perception (Section IV) in animals to examples of work in AI. These problems are typical of those raised within "cognitive ethology", a term recently coined to cover studies of the psychological competence of animals [Griffin, 1978], such as the work on chimps directed by D. Premack or D. M. Rumbaugh. Finally, in Section V, I discuss three common objections to computer models of intelligence: the difficulty of validating such models by experiments; the architectural difference between brains and digital computers; and the problem of ascribing conscious phenomenology to animals.

II. *AI as the Study of Representation*

Years ago, I saw in the pages of *Punch* a cartoon more memorable than most (I have redrawn it in *Figure 1*). It showed a kingfisher sitting on a willow-branch, staring at a fish in the river below, and thinking to itself, "$\mu = \sin \varnothing / \sin \vartheta$." This cartoon is no mere triviality, for it is a reminder of some deeply puzzling questions.

How does the kingfisher manage to catch the fish, no matter (within limits) where it is in the water? Unlike some birds, it does not dive vertically into the water, nor does it pursue the fish while under water. Kingfishers are plunge-divers, who go rapidly straight to the target. Given that the kingfisher has never heard of Snell's law, does it have to go through some alternative process of computation to adjust its angle-of-dive appropriately— and if so, what? A less obvious puzzle is how the bird manages to identify part of the scene as a fish, or as food, in the first place, and how it is thereupon led to take appropriate action (that is, how does it know that it should dive, irrespective of how steep the dive should be)?

Figure 1

All these puzzles concern the information being used by the animal, and the way in which the animal is using it. One might expect, then, that AI should be somehow relevant. AI is a recent branch of information-science that is suited to the needs of ethology or theoretical psychology because it defines a wide range of qualitatively distinct and structurally complex symbolic representations and interpretative procedures. The computational concepts used in AI are concerned with the reception, storage, transformation, interpretation, and use of information by information-processing systems which employ and construct symbols—and symbol-manipulation procedures—of many distinct kinds.

It is often regarded as problematic whether or not animals have mental representations, or use symbolic systems or languages. Sometimes it is even stated categorically that they do not. Piaget, for example, says that animals (like newborn babies) do not have representations, and Chomsky denies that even chimps enjoy language. To some degree, these disputes turn on terminological differences in the use of terms such as "representation" and "language". But even setting aside such terminological differences, it remains true that whether or not any animals employ symbolic representations is widely regarded as doubtful.

The lesson of AI is that many animals must have representations enabling them to interpret stimulus-information sensibly in widely differing contexts and to take appropriate action accordingly. The more flexible the action, the more complex must be the computational resources for monitoring, planning, and scheduling different types of activity. In particular, when the creature has to take account of a wide range of *structural* differences and similarities between distinct situations (as opposed to concentrating on only one or a few physical parameters), these structural features can only be represented *symbolically*—for, by hypothesis, they have no *physical* features in common.

It does not follow, of course, that the representations in animals' brains are comparable in detail to the symbol-manipulating processes in current digital computers (in which representations are coded at distinct, and often physically separated, locations in the machine). Indeed, some of the most interesting recent work in AI, and in computationally-based psychology, focuses on *connectionist* systems, in which extensive parallel-processing allows for a representation to be *distributed* across an entire network of computational units. [Hinton & Anderson, 1981; Rumelhart & McClelland, 1986]. I shall say a little about such systems below, but—since the vast majority of AI-work has not been of this type—most of the computer-models I shall mention are conceptualized in terms of (as well as being implemented in) digital computers.

That animals need to employ (computational mechanisms functioning as) abstract, symbolic, representations is true *irrespective* of whether the animal is able also to communicate with its conspecifics, by warning-cries, mating-calls, and the like. And it is true whether or not the animals is able, like humans, to employ a syntactically structured public language, using units of meaning whose semantic import is determined by social conventions rather than by fixed genetic mechanisms. The point of present importance is that even much *noncommunicative* behaviour has to be understood in computational terms such that internal symbolic processes must be attributed to the creature. Indeed, the interpretation of audible or visible signs, words, or gestures *as* communications with a certain meaning presupposes the computational mechanisms involved in sensory perception in general. This is why one AI-worker has referred to "the primacy of non-communicative language" [Sloman, 1979].

This is not to say that *all* computations carried out by animals are effected symbolically. For example, hoverflies appear to compute their interception paths with conspecifics according to a simply specifiable rule, one which could plausibly be "hard-wired" into the flies' brains [Collett & Land, 1978]. Although this rule *could* be represented and applied within a symbolic system, it is reasonable to suggest that it has been "learnt" by the evolutionary process, and is embodied in the flies' neurophysiology. It is significant, however, that the computations concerned are relatively inflexible: the fly in effect assumes that the size and velocity of the target are *always* those corresponding to hoverflies, and on this rigid (and fallible) basis the creature determines its angle of turn, when initiating its flight, according to the variable approach angle subtended by the target. Moreover, the fly's path cannot be adjusted in mid-flight, there being no way in which the pursuer can be influenced by feedback from the (perhaps unpredictable) movement of the target animal.

This rigid behaviour is fairly common in insects, but the higher animals are capable of considerable flexibility in adjusting their behaviour to widely differing (and continuously changing) circumstances, where the relevant "parameters" are structural features rather than physical ones (such as angle-of-approach). The *visual* capacities of the higher animals are typically more flexible also: for instance, many species can discriminate the position, shape, texture, and surface-orientation of arbitrarily many physical objects—even objects seen for the very first time. Recent computational work in "low-level" vision—an example of which is discussed below—shows that these capacities, even though they are largely hardwired (innate), cannot be understood unless they are conceptualized as involving (multi-levelled) representational processes [Mayhew & Frisby, 1984; Marr, 1982].

The term "cognitive ethology" is only recently coined, but the problems are not new. In his seminal paper on "the invisible worlds of animals and men", Jacob von Uexkull [1934] showed that the task of a cognitive ethology is to articulate the varied *Umwelten* or different species. To do this, we need to ask what a given species can perceive, and what it can do accordingly. Those aspects of environment or action which a creature does not have the epistemological resources to represent, cannot form part of its cognitive world.

Von Uexkull illustrated these points by his unforgettable pictures of the living-room as seen by fly, dog, or man, and of the fish and the boat as seen by a sea-urchin. But, charming though they are, his pictures do not clearly articulate the similarities and differences between the invisible worlds of these species. Work in AI might help us to a richer understanding of such matters, as I shall now try to show by reference to examples concerning the planning of action and the perception of the physical world.

III. *Computational Concepts in the Explanation of Action*

The concept of purposive action has often entered ethological discussion. Purposive action is behaviour controlled by a guiding representation of some desired state, whose overall plan allows for obstacles to be overcome by appropriate variations in the activities selected as means to the end (notice that this is an essentially *psychological* definition, so that purposive behaviour is *not* the same as behaviour controlled by feedback of the sort studied in classical cybernetics or control-theory) [Boden, 1972]. To be sure, ethologists in the past have been more concerned to deny the relevance of this concept to animal behaviour than to insist on its applicability. Thus in 1937 Konrad Lorenz criticized anthropomorphic attributions of "instinct", saying that "To assume a 'whole-producing,' directive instinct superior to all part reactions could evidently be justified only if the effects of a regulative factor, exceeding the experimentally demonstrable regulative faculty of the single reaction, could be observed" [Lorenz, 1937, p. 157].

Since then, entomologists and ornithologists in particular have often identified independently controlled units of behaviour, which in normal circumstances combine to give the appearance of activity that is planned as a whole and dependent on a recognition of complex means-end relationships. D.S. Lehrman's [1955; 1958 (a & b)] studies of parental behaviour in ring-doves are an example of this sort of analysis. Various hormonal factors and several "social" releasing stimuli interact, so that the behaviour of birds and squabs is reciprocally determined in an appropriate manner. But if the normal sequence is upset the doves do not engage in variation of means, they do not adapt their behaviour intelligently so as to achieve the desirable (though evidently not *desired*) end-state of a nestful of happy, healthy chicks. (It does not follow, of course, that ring-doves never engage in behaviour guided by desires, nor that the independent parts of the "parental" sequence are not flexible to some degree according to circumstances: but the guiding goal of *rearing healthy chicks* cannot be posited as an explanation of this sequence.)

Recently, however, primatologists have begun to ask whether the behaviour of apes, at least, may sometimes be directed by plans or strategies guided by an idea of the goal. And some ethologists raise this question also about non-primate, and even non-mammalian, species such as beavers and bees [Premack & Woodruff, 1978; Griffin, 1978; Savage-Rumbaugh, Rumbaugh, & Boysen, 1978]. But it is generally agreed even by those willing to consider such questions, that they are very difficult to answer. This difficulty rests partly in the fact that psychology has not provided a theoretical vocabulary for expressing the stucture of purposive activity. Indeed, for many years Anglo-Saxon psychologists actively discouraged any such endeavour, because of the anti-mentalistic bias of behaviourism. AI may be helpful here, for there are already a large number of AI programs concerned with planning, in which are defined procedures of varying complexity for comparing current with desired state and selecting activities accordingly [Charniak & McDermott, 1984, ch. 9; Boden, 1987, ch. 12]. The computational concepts involved offer the beginning of theoretical taxonomy of plans. Such a taxonomy could aid the behavioural analysis of those forms of animal activity that are apparently purposive, rather than being simply "automatic" or "mechanical" in nature. In a recent publication, Lorenz [1977] has cited examples arguing that this is a continuous range rather than a bipolar distinction within animal behaviour. Indeed, it might better be described as a multidimensional space. Computational considerations could help distinguish the different points in the space of actual (and, ideally, of possible) behaviours.

Many actions of insects are sequential patterns of invariant order which, once started, are "automatically" executed to the bitter end even in inappropriate circumstances. Sometimes there is a degree of flexibility due to local conditions (such as the configuration of the terrain), but there is no feedback of information capable of altering the overall pattern; at best, it can be interrupted, cut short without the possibility of restarting later at the same point. And some other examples of animal action (such as the parental behaviour of Lehrman's ring-doves) are composed of units which follow "mechanically" in a fixed order provided that at each point the relevant releasing stimulus occurs.

AI-plans are not like this, although most people unfamiliar with AI assume that they are. They are hierarchically organized wholes, variable according to circumstance. Many programs have a "heterarchical" control-structure, in which control is widely distributed throughout the system: the sub-programs on various levels can communicate up and down *and sideways*, so that decisions can be taken at a local level relatively independently of the overall goal of the system as a whole. This type of control-structure (which is often compared to a human committee of experts) makes it easier to effect subtle variations according to context, so that what at a higher level is clearly "one and the same plan" can be interpreted in importantly different ways on different occasions. Various sorts of monitoring activity are employed to schedule different sorts of action and to make adjustments to ongoing action that is not proceeding (in its relation to the problem-environment) as well as it might be.

For example, some programs monitor and adjust the execution of their plans by reference to their internal representation of the preconditions and consequences of different actions. Thus the mobile robot SHAKEY, while executing a plan for moving blocks from one room to another, asks itself at each step whether the plan as executed so far has produced the expected results (which it may not have done if the environment has changed unexpectedly); what portion of the plan needs to be executed next (which may not be the portion initially foreseen, if the previous question was answered in the negative); and whether this next portion can indeed be executed in the current state of the world (if not, a subgoal may be set up to realize the necessary preconditions) [Fikes, Hart, & Nilsson, 1972]. Other planning programs exist with a richer representational power and so a greater flexibility of action. Some can choose in a principled fashion whether or not to commit themselves to a specific ordering of subgoals ahead of time, and accordingly decide sensibly when the time comes to execute the plan. Some can generate an outline plan that omits all reference to detail, and translate this outline into detailed effective action when necessary [Sacerdoti, 1974]. Some can anticipate unwanted side-effects and modify the plan accordingly, so as to avoid them or neutralize their unwelcome aspects [Sussman, 1975]. Some can envisage different alternative strategies for achieving a goal, and use both reasoning and empirical enquiry in choosing between them. Some can recognize a *cul-de-sac* and re-enter a strategy at the precise point where it was previously abandoned, possibly generating a new mini-plan for overcoming the local obstacle which (as it remembers) led to its abandonment in the first place [Fahlman, 1974]. And some can construct a representation of the goals and plan-following of another program, using it to guide interaction between the two systems [Power, 1979].

Were one to apply the insights gained in the development of these programs to the experiments on chimps done by D. Premack and G. Woodruff, or by D. M. Rumbaugh and colleagues, one would be led to ask a number of questions not mentioned by them. For example, how sensitive are chimps to constraints on the temporal ordering of certain units of behaviour in the context of an overall problem such that *this* sub-unit has to be performed before *that* one? (They clearly are sensitive to such constraints in some degree, since they will often go to fetch a tool before attempting to do the task for which the tool is required.) Does a chimp have the representational complexity to gather together two or three tools, each of which will be needed in the ensuing task? Or must the chimp think about only one step at a time? If it sees another individual attempting the second step before trying the first (where this ordering is mandatory), can the chimp realize and communicate the information that the required step should be taken instead? If a chimp decides to abandon a task, what features influence its decision? Is it capable of coming back to that task at an appropriate moment, and if so can it remember where it was in the task previously, or must it begin again from scratch? Does a chimp ever engage in activity which looks as though it is a preparation for some later task, either in establishing necessary preconditions or in forestalling unwelcome consequences that would otherwise ensue on later performance of the task in question? If a chimp is interrupted during its problem-solving by some irrelevant occurrence, does it remember the unfinished task, and does it remember what stage it had reached at the time of interruption? And so one, and so on. We must not merely ask whether chimps generate representations of plans, but must distinguish the computationally different types of plan that they might be using in the control of their behaviour, and that they might be attributing to other individuals (whether chimp or human).

Some AI-workers would echo Lorenz at this point, objecting that one cannot assume that apparently integrated behaviour is controlled by some integrally organized plan, or that flexible, context-sensitive behaviour is guided by a representation of the desired overall result. They would refer to programs called "productive systems", in which control rests in a number of largely independent rules, each of which may be acquired in isolation, and each of which expresses a Condition-Action pair. Each rule tests for a certain Condition (in input or in short-term memory) and then carries out the relevant Action (either producing output or altering the contents of short-term memory). This approach is quite different in spirit from the "planning" approach previously described. It is better able to represent the continual shifting of the focus of attention, and also the interruption of behaviour, whereby appropriate action can be instantly taken on the occurrence of an unexpected event. Yet it can model problem-solving behaviour which one might have thought to be controlled by a plan explicitly representing the structure of the task as a whole. However, this purposive structure has to be implicit in the system if it is to model hierarchically integrated behaviour. So, for example, constraints have to be written into the content of the rules, or the priority and/or temporal ordering of the rules have to be constrained, in ways that decrease the independence of the several rules and so go against the spirit of the approach in its pure form [Davis & King, 1977].

Production systems can sometimes be matched to detailed behavioural protocols, and studied *pari passu* with experimental results. For example, a system of rules whose subsets generate different patterns of seriation (staircase-building) can be matched to children's motor and verbal behaviour so as to capture a wide range of detailed observations [Young, 1976]; and a production system for subtraction can model the many commonly observed errors in subtraction sums that children make [Young, 1977]. These examples show that even a small number of production rules can give rise to performance that is considerably more varied and flexible than the relentless formula-following common in insects or the successive behaviour-triggering seen in Lehrman's ring-doves. And large production systems, incorporating many hundreds of rules, can generate problem-solving performance comparable to subtle and complex human behaviour.

It may be that much animal behaviour, especially non-mammalian forms, could fruitfully be modelled in these terms. For the Condition may be an external environmental condition (temperature, sunrise, or the presence of a fish or a cat), a state of the animals' internal environment (hormonal concentration), or an inner psychological condition (such as the impulse or desire to catch a fish). And the Action may be motor behaviour (as in diving for the fish or fleeing the cat), or psychological processing (as in activating the desire to catch a fish, or checking to see whether it is on the surface or deep in the water). Ethologists might find it useful to try to write production systems modelling behaviour in different species, and to enquire into the acquisition (whether genetic or through learning) of individual rules. Running one's set of rules on a computer enables one to test not only their coherence but their implications, for one can systematically omit or alter individual rules and observe the performance so generated. In this way, one might enrich one's understanding of what Lorenz termed "the experimentally demonstrable regulative faculty of the single reactions".

The early robot SHAKEY, as its name implies, was not impressive considered as a *motor* system: its interest was in its capacity to plan and monitor its actions. Recent work in robotics recognizes that motor action involves not only trajectory planning, but detailed movement-control, maintenance of stability, calculation of forces, and visuomotor coordination. One might think that only the first of these (planning) involves artificial intelligence: the others, it seems, are mere engineering. However, the engineering is not "mere" at all: very difficult theoretical problems are involved in (for example) controlling jointed robot-manipulators with the degrees of freedom of the human hand [Hardy, 1984]. Likewise, enabling a camera-equipped robot to *avoid* the obstacles it sees in its (potential) path is no simple matter. Work in robotics is increasingly grounded in the detailed theory of mechanics and dynamics, in roboticists' attempts to develop computational procedures that can exploit this knowledge in performing practical tasks. The crucial theoretical problems have not all been identified, still less solved (today's commercial robots avoid these problems, but only by compromising their flexibility). But because the basic information-processing task involved in motor action is common to robotics and motor-psychology alike, theoretically-grounded work in robotics can be expected to move nearer to work in motor-physiology and motor-psychology.

IV. *Computational Concepts in the Understanding of Perception*
    Coordinated with its active aspect (whether this be regulated by an overall plan or by isolable rules), the *Umwelt* of any animal has a perceptual aspect. For example, many species are assumed by ethologists to enjoy motion-perception and object-concepts of some sort. Just what sort, however, is usually unclear. Even in the human case, the psychological processes underlying motion-perception are not fully understood.
    Some recent computer-modelling work done by Shimon Ullman [1979] suggests computational questions and hypothetical answers that are relevant not only to human vision (Ullman's prime focus), but to animal vision also. Like the psychologist J. J. Gibson [1979], Ullman attempts to show that many perceptual features can be recognized by relatively low-level psychophysiological mechanisms, whose functioning relies on the informa-

tion available in the ambient light rather than on high-level concepts or cerebral schemata. But unlike Gibson, who posits a "direct" unanalysable perceptual process of "information pickup", Ullman views this functioning as a significantly complex process intelligible in computational terms.

Ullman reminds us that if two differing views or input-arrays are successively presented to the visual system, then one of several phenomenologically distinct perceptions my arise. We may see an object (visible in the earlier view) disappearing, and being *replaced* by another one—as in a game of "peekaboo"; we may see one and the same (rigid) object *moving*, perhaps involving a change in its appearance due to rotation; we may see one and the same object *changing* in shape so as to be transformed into something different—as the baby that Alice was holding gradually turned into a pig before her eyes; finally, we may see an object moving and changing shape at the same time (as does a walking mammal). Using the experimental technique of "apparent movement" (which, interestingly, has been shown to occur in some animal species [Smith, 1941; Rock, Tauber, & Heller, 1964, 1966]), the conditions under which these perceptions are elicited can be empirically investigated.

Ullman's project is to discover the series of computations that the visual system performs on the input-pairs so as to arrive at an interpretation of the (2-D) array in terms of (3-D) replacement, motion, or change. In particular, he asks whether (and *how*) these distinct percepts can be differentially generated without assuming reliance on high-level concepts of specific 3-D objects (such as fish or sticklebacks), and even without assuming the prior recognition of a specific overall shape (such as a sort of narrow pointed ellipse with sharp projections on its upper surface). As the ethologists might put it, Ullman attempts to follow Lloyd Morgan's Canon, in asking what are the *minimal* computational processes that need to be posited to explain motion-perception. As we shall see, Ullman is misled by his concentration on mathematically minimal computations into assuming a specific hypothesis which is ethologically implausible—but this does not destroy the general interest of his approach.

As regards the visual interpretation of each array considered in isolation, Ullman relies on the work of D. C. Marr [1982]. Marr studied the information potentially available in the ambient light falling on the retina, and the image-interpreting computations performed on it by peripheral levels of the visual system. He is largely responsible for the insight, mentioned above, that even low-level vision has to be understood as a *representational* process—one in which the visual organism constructs a series of representations on successive levels, culminating in an object-centered (view-independent) 3-D description of the object in question. ("Low-level" vision involves the interpretation of the 2-D input, or intensity array, in terms of 3-D properties of physical surfaces/objects; "high-level" vision involves the recognition of specific categories of objects, and the use of expectations and concepts to guide the process of visual interpretation.)

The first state of visual computation, according the Marr, is the formation of a "Primal Sketch", an image consisting of descriptions of the scene in terms of features like *shading-edge, extended-edge, line,* and *blob* (which vary as to *fuzziness, contrast, lightness, position, orientation, size,* and *termination* points). These epistemological primitives are the putative result of preprocessing of the original intensity array at the retinal level—that is, they are not computations performed by the visual cortex (still less, the cerebral cortex). Marr defines further computations on these primitive descriptions, which group lines, points, and blobs together in various ways, resulting in the separation of figure and ground. He stresses that these perceptual computations *construct* the image, which is a symbolic description (or articulated representation) of the scene based on the initial stimulus-array. The computations are thus interpretative processes, carried out by the visual system considered as a symbol-manipulating system rather than simply as a physical transducer (though Marr attempts to ground his computational hypotheses in specific facts of visual psychophysiology).

Starting with Marr's basic meaningful units, Ullman defines further visual computations which would enable the system, presented with two differing views, to make a perceptual decision between replacement, motion, or change. Ullman divides the computational problem faced by the visual system into two logically distinct parts, which he calls the *correspondence* and the *interpretation* problems. (The latter term unfortunately obscures the fact that *all* these computations, including Marr's, are interpretative processes, carried out by the visual system in its role as a symbol-manipulative device.)

The correspondence problem is to indentify specific portions of the changing image as representing the same object at different times. This identity-computation must succeed if the final perception is to be that of a single object, whether in motion or in change. Conversely, the perception of replacement presupposes that no such identity could be established at the correspondence stage. The interpretation problem is to identify parts of the input arrays as representing objects, with certain 3-D shapes, and moving through 3-space (if they are moving) in a specific way. In principle, correspondence and interpretation-computations together can distinguish between the three types of perception in question. And, if specific hypothetical examples of such computations are to be of any interest to students of biological organisms, they should be able to distinguish reliably (though not necessarily infallibly) between equivalent changes in the real-world environment.

The last point is relevant to the way in which Ullman defines specific correspondence-and-interpretation algorithms. In principle, any part of one 2-D view could correspond with (be an appearance of the same object as) many different parts of another; similarly, any 2-D view has indefinitely many possible 3-D interpretations. (Anyone who doubts this should recall the images facing them in distorting mirrors at funfairs.) Faced with this difficulty, Ullman makes specific assumptions about normal viewing conditions, and takes into account certain physical and geometrical properties of the real world, as well as (human) psychological evidence based on studies of apparent motion. Accordingly, he formulates a hypothetical set of computational constraints which he claims will both assess the degree of match between two views so as to choose the better one, and typically force a 3-D interpretation which is both unique and veridical. For instance, for the correspondence stage he defines "affinity functions" that compute the degree of match between two points or short line-segments, depending on their distance, brightness, retinal position, inter-stimulus (time) intervals, length, and orientation. And for the interpretation stage, he defines a way of computing the shape and motion of a rigid object from three views of it, making his system assume that if such a computation succeeds then it is indeed faced with a rigid body in motion (as opposed to two different objects or one object changing its shape). He justifies this by proving mathematically that, except in highly abnormal viewing conditions, three views of a rigid object can uniquely determine its shape and motion.

Given that Ullman's computations can indeed interpret correspondence, shape, and motion in a wide range of paired 2-D views (which can be tested by running his system in it programmed form on a computer provided with the relevant input), what are we to say about the ethological importance of his work?

The first thing to notice is that Ullman embodies implicit assumptions about the physics and geometry of the real world, and about biologically normal viewing conditions, into computations carried out by the visual system. It is plausible that many species may have evolved such implicit computational constraints. That is, the animal's mind may implicitly embody knowledge about its external environment, which knowledge is used by it in its perceptual interpretations. Something of the sort seems to be true for migratory birds, who have some practical grasp of the earth's magnetic field or of stellar constellations; and, as I shall suggest presently, the kingfisher may have some practical grasp of the refractive properties of water.

What is ethologically implausible about Ullman's hypotheses is not that they embody some knowledge about material objects and normal viewing conditions, but rather that they assume the perception of *rigid* objects to be basic, while perception of non-rigid movement is taken to be a more complex special case. *Mathematically*, of course, the perception of non-rigid motion is more complex; but this does not prove that it is *biologically* secondary to the perception of rigid objects. At least in the higher animals, it is more likely that the visual perception of shape and motion have evolved in response to such biologically significant environment features as the gait or stance of hunter or prey, or the facial grimaces and tail-waving of conspecifics. The fact that human beings do not always perceive the correct (rigid) structure when presented with a mathematically adequate though impoverished stimulus, may be due not (as Ullman suggests) to their failing to pick up all the mathematically necessary information in the stimulus, but rather to their using computational strategies evolved for the perception of non-rigid objects which— *even* when directed at rigid objects—need more information than is present in the experimental stimulus concerned [Sloman, 1980; cf. Ullman, 1980]. Admittedly, a robot could be provided with an Ullmanesque capacity to perceive rigid objects in motion; but whether any creature on the phylogenetic scale employs such visual mechanisms is another questions.

Our friend the kingfisher apparently possesses computational mechanisms which can discover the real position of a fish at varying depths in the water. Ullman's general approach suggests that these could well be relatively low-level processes, not requiring cerebral computations (as puzzling out Snell's law presumably does). For the visual computations algorithmically defined by Ullman do not depend on high-level processes capable of identifying (recognizing) objects as members of a specific class: the system does not need to know that an object is a fish, or even that it has the 3-D shape that it has, in order to know that it is an object. Nor does it need any familiarity with the object; that is, it does not need to have experienced those two views in association beforehand. Ullman therefore suggest (*contra* empiricists and Piaget) that a baby—or, one might add, a kingfisher—can see that two appearances are views of one and the same object even if it has never seen the sort of object before, and even if it has no tactile or manipulative evidence suggesting that they pertain to one and the same thing. These conclusions follow from the fact that all of the correspondence-computation, and much of the interpretation-computation, is via low-level, autonomous processes that do not depend on recognition of the input as a familiar 3-D object. The correspondence-computations match primitive elements (those defined by Marr) in successive views, and do not depend on computations of the overall shape as a whole.

It follows that creatures incapable of computing shape in any detail, or of recognizing different classes of physical object, may nonetheless be able to compute motion. As the example of von Uexkull's sea-urchin suggests, this is no news to ethologists, who often have behavioural evidence that an animal can perceive motion though they doubt its ability to be aware of detailed shapes. But Ullman's achievement is to have complemented this empirically-based intuition by a set of admirably clear hypotheses about precisely what visual computations may be involved, at least in the human case. That some of his hypotheses are biologically dubious does not destroy the ethological interest of his general approach.

Ullman's work also casts some light on our kingfisher-cartoon. For if the general shape, the location, and the motion of objects can be computed in a low-level, autonomous fashion, then it is not impossible that a kingfisher may possess comparable perceptual mechanisms capable of computing the depth of a fish in water. The refractive index of water would be implicitly embodied in these computational mechanisms, perhaps in an unalterable fashion. So a kingfisher experimentally required to dive into oil might starve to death, like newborn chicks provided with distorting goggles that shift the light five degrees to the right, who never learn to peck for grains of corn in the right place [Hess, 1956]. This assumes (what is the case for the chicks), that the kingfisher utilizes an inborn visuomotor coordination, linking the perceptual and active aspects of its *Umwelt*, a coordination that is not only innate but unalterable. Psychological experiments on human beings, and comparable studies of chimps, show that these species by contrast can learn to adjust to some systematic distortions of the physics of the visual field [Stratton, 1896, 1897; Kohler, 1962].

In their paper asking whether chimps are lay psychologists, Premack and Woodruff remark in an aside that one might also enquire whether they are lay physicists. Before being in a position to do this at any level of detail, one will need a clearer sense of what the content of lay physics might possibly be. The foregoing discussion of Ullman's work suggests some part of the answer, in articulating assumptions about the physics and geometry of 3-D objects viewed in air (and, perhaps, in water) that my inform the *Umwelten* at least of some animals. But, presumably, human beings and many other species possess many more concepts and inferential structures that embody everyday knowledge of the material worked, much of which knowledge may be acquired through learning. Some work in AI, which admittedly is programmatic rather than programmed, is an interesting preliminary attack on this problem [Hayes, 1979, 1985; Bobrow, 1985]).

In his "Naive Physics Manifesto", P. J. Hayes [1979, 1985] asks how one might construct a formalization of our everyday knowledge of the physical world. Ethologists may be tempted to dismiss such an enquiry as irrelevant to their problems: human beings have Newton and Einstein, whereas animals do not, so human knowledge of physics cannot be relevant to enquiries about chimps, beavers, or bees. That this would be an inappropriate objection is evident from the fact that the *Punch* cartoon I mentioned earlier would have been almost as funny if it had figured a human fisherman rather than a kingfisher. Not only do we not usually think of Snell's law when we try to net a fish or tickle a trout, but we could not use it to help us to do so even if we did. Similarly, we do not balance a bicycle by applying the formulae of mathematical dynamics. Our everyday intuition of concepts such as *weight, support, velocity, height, inside/outside, next to, boundary, path, entrance, obstacle, fluid, and cause* (to name but a few) are pretheoretical. It is this pretheoretical knowledge which interests Hayes.

It is apparent that some animals share much of this pretheoretical knowledge with us—often, as in the case of the kingfisher, also knowing things which we do not. (Though in some cases "pretheoretical knowledge" may be grounded in a small number of independent condition-action rules, corresponding broadly to Gibson's notion of perceptual "affordances", rather than in prelinguistic conceptual networks of the sort posited by Hayes.) A cat or monkey leaping from wall to wall, or branch to branch, needs some representation of *support* and *stability*, and diving animals need some grasp to the difference between *solids* and *fluids*, as well as of *depth, movement,* and *distance.* Chimps clearly have some grasp of notions such as *inside, obstacle, place* . . . . . We will not be in a position to ascertain how much grasp, of which concepts, until we are clearer about the nature of these concepts in our own case. And this means knowing the perceptual evidence in which the concepts are anchored and the motor activities which test for them or which are carried out on the basis of conditional tests defined in terms of them. For example, newborn creatures who refuse to cross a "visual cliff" apparently have some innate procedure for recognizing the absence of *support,* where the object to be supported is their own body. It does not follow that they understand in any sense that the bottom bricks of a tower support the top ones—although this is something which a leaping animal living in a jungle or an untidy house may have to learn. To understand a concept involves having some representation of the inferences that can usefully be drawn to link it with other concepts in the same general domain. *Support,* for instance, has something to do with *above* for leaping creatures who can recognize the potential for action in a pile of bricks. Hayes outlines some ways in which the core concepts of naive physics, and groups of cognate concepts, may be organized, so that inferential paths can be traced between them. His work is an intriguing beginning of a very important enterprise, which should help us understand *how* perceptual experience functions in the control of motor action.

A word of warning is in order here, however. Hayes is primarily interested in the human *Umwelt,* which is informed through and through by natural language. It is true that our earliest knowledge of naive physics is prelinguistic: the baby's sensorimotor understanding is prior to her acquisition of English or French. But it follows from Hayes' account of meaning that, once such natural languages are acquired, the meaning of the more primitive core concepts is altered—not merely added to. In principle, even if we had a precise account of adult human knowledge of *inside, support,* and *behind,* we could not equate any part of this with the chimp's knowledge simply by jettisoning those parts of it influenced by our linguistic representations. Rather, we would need to be able to trace the development of our naive physical concepts, distinguishing their earlier, sensorimotor forms from the later, linguistically-informed, semantic contents and inferential patterns. Hayes makes some relevant remarks, but even more apposite here is the computationally-informed work of the psycholinguists G. A. Miller and P. N. Johnson-Laird, who have studied the basic perceptual procedures in which our linguistic abilities are grounded [Miller & Johnson-Laird, 1976].

Miller and Johnson-Laird define a number of perceptual discriminations in detailed procedural terms, utilizing what is known about our sensorimotor equipment and development. They then show how these discriminatory procedures could come to function as the semantic anchoring of our lexicon. For example, perceptual predicates that can be procedurally defined include the following spatial descriptions: x is higher than y; the distance from x to y is zero; x is in front of the moving object y; y is between x and z; x has boundary y; x is convex; x is changing shape; x has the exterior surface y; x is included spatially in y; x, y, and z lie in a straight line; x travels along the path p. They give both psychological and physiological evidence for the primacy of these notions, and they use them to define object-recognizing routines of increasing power. Their sensitivity to computational issues leads them to ask not only *which* predicates are involved in a certain judgement, but *when* each predicate is applied in the judgmental process. (For exampie, the logically equivalent "y over x" and "x under y" are not psychologically equivalent: the first term in the relation should designate the thing whose location is to be determined, while the second should represent the immobile landmark that can be used to determine it.) The perceptual routines they define as the meaning of words such as "in", "on", "outside", and "at" are surprisingly complex.

Were a chimp to grasp the meaning of "in" or "on" in Ameslan, therefore, this would presuppose extremely complex perceptual computations on the chimp's part. And animals which, unlike chimps, have no great manipulative ability, would not be able to compute those perceptual discriminations requiring motor activities such as putting bananas inside boxes, so that their understanding of naive physics would be correspondingly impoverished. Von Holst's [1954] studies of reafference, and Hein and Held's [1963] experiments on visual development in kittens, suggested that many perceptual discriminations require active bodily movement: insofar as this is so, the creature could not substitute an understanding of "putting in" derived merely from watching others. (It is perhaps worth remarking that limbless thalidomide babies apparently reach a normal understanding of physical concepts: whether their natural language plays an essential part in enabling them to do so is not known.) Irrespective of chimps' potential mastery of Ameslan, the implication common to the work of Ullman, Marr, Hayes, and Miller and Johnson-Laird is that the perceptual and motor abilities of animals far lower in the phylogenetic scale than chimps must be based on representational competences of a highly complex kind. So an increased sensitivity to computational issues might help ethologists to investigate the symbol-manipulations carried out by different species, and to compare *Umwelten* in a systematic fashion.

In addition to empirical observations (about which, more in the following section), it may be that general results in the abstract theory of computation might help in this systematic comparison. If it could be shown, for example, that a given type of representation in principle could not express a certain type of information, or that it would be computationally enormously less efficient than some other type of representation, such insights might help guide the ethologist in attributing specific representational capacities to different animals.

For instance, abstract considerations show that computational mechanisms of a certain type (namely, "perceptrons", of which an example would be a nervous net with no significant prior structure) simply cannot achieve specific kinds of learning or spatial pattern recognition [Minsky & Papert, 1969]. Since it is abundantly clear that animal brains do have a significant prior structure, this result is somewhat academic from the point of view of the ethologist. But other results of this general type might be more relevant.

For example, in discussing what F. Rosenblatt [1958] had termed "perceptrons", M. L. Minsky and S. Papert [1969] claimed to show that certain mechanisms capable of performing some nontrivial computations are incapable of performing others which at first sight might appear to be within their range. Perceptrons are parallel-processing devices which make decisions on the basis of weighted evidence from many local operators, and various physiological examples have been suggested by cybernetically-inclined neurophysiologists interested in pattern-recognition and "self-organizing systems." Minksy and Papert sought to show, by way of abstract considerations alone, that no simple perceptron (without loops or feedback paths) could compute spatial connectedness, though it could compute convexity. Similarly, they claimed that no system without significant prior structure could in practice learn discriminations of high complexity, even given the existence of feedback paths.

Likewise, current work on "connectionist" systems (networks of parallel-processing units, wherein a representation is embodied by the *pattern* of excitation distributed across the network) has explored a number of different types of such systems: deterministic or stochastic, binary-valued or continuous. It has been proved, for example, that a certain sort of network (called a "Boltzmann machine" because it consists of stochastic units whose behaviour can be described by the equations of thermodynamics) can learn to represent *any* structure, given infinite time [Ackley, Hinton, & Sejnowski, 1985; Hinton & Sejnowski, 1986]. In practice, however, most real learning-problems (since they involve significant levels of noise) cannot be solved in a reasonable time by Boltzmann machines.

Clearly, results such as these are relevant to the representational capacity of nervous systems of different kinds, whether in the form of more or less complex nervous nets or of highly structured cerebral systems. Whether these abstract considerations can soon be brought into articulation with specific neurophysiological data is another question, since in only very few cases can we realistically hope to have an adequate (still less, complete) understanding of the neural connections within an entire nervous system.

Another suggestive example of abstract work that might throw light on issues of interest to ethologists is provided by John McCarthy [McCarthy & Hayes, 1969]. McCarthy has long been interested in the representation of basic epistemological concepts (such as those discussed by his student, Hayes), and has recently embarked on what he terms "meta-epistemology", the attempt to define general representational or computational constraints on the sorts of mechanisms in principle capable of grasping particular notions. (The account of perceptrons was in fact an early example of meta-epistemology, but was not conceived as part of an integrated research-programme directed to a wide range of representational systems.)

Again, A. Sloman [1978a, pp. 144–176] has shown that "analogical" representations may be in various ways more computationally efficient than "Fregean" ones. He defines an analogical representation as one in which there is some significant correspondence between the structure of the representation and the structure of the thing represented. By contrast, a Fregean representation need have no such correspondence, since the structure of the representation reflects not the structure of the thing itself, but the structure of the procedure (thought process) by which that thing is identified. To understand a Fregean representation is to know how to interpret it so as to establish what it is referring to, basically by the method described by the logician Frege as applying *functions* to *arguments*. Analogical representations, however, are understood or interpreted by matching the two structures concerned (that is, of the representation itself and of the domain represented), and their associated inference-procedures, in a systematic way. Applying this distinction to our kingfisher cartoon, for example, the formula expressing Snell's law is a Fregean representation, whereas the diagram itself (with the lines representing the paths of light and constructing the relevant angles) is an analogical representation.

An example of the use—and usefulness—of analogical representation has been provided by B. V. Funt [1980], who has followed Sloman's suggestions by programming a system that can reason from visual diagrams. Funt utilizes the 2-D space inherent in the hardware of the machine as an analogue of 2-D paper, so that a diagram is embodied in the machine as a certain state of a 2-D visual array, or "retina". The system's task, given a diagram like that of *Figure 2*, is to discover whether the arrangement of blocks depicted is stable, and—if it is not—to predict the movements (falling, sliding, motion ended by contact with another block) and the final state of the various blocks. The answers to these questions are discovered from the diagram (given certain simple diagrammatic transformations carried out by the system, which are structurally analogous to changes that would happen in the real world), rather than being computed in terms of abstract mathematical equations and specific numerical values.

Previous programs that could recognize stability or instability of putative block-structures did so by computing sophisticated equations of physics and quantitative parameters, and one such program (one of the planning programs previously mentioned)

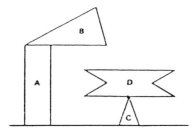

Figure 2

needed over 80% of its computational resources for these calculations alone [Fahlman, 1974]. What is more, those programs
were unable to predict the specific structural changes that would
follow on an instability. But, much as it is "obvious" to us from
the diagram (though not from a verbal or mathematical description of the same state-of-affairs) that B will hit D, that D will then
tilt with its left half moving downwards, and that B will end up
touching both A and D but *not* the ground, so it is easily discov-
erable by Funt's program that this is what will happen.

Briefly, the program "imagines" gradual changes in the position of the blocks by exploiting the 2-D nature of the retina in
which the diagram is embodied. So for instance it imagines
gradually moving an unstable block (such as B) downwards,
pivoting on the relevant point of support. It studies "snapshots"
of the successive positions, and so discovers specific points of
contact with coincidentally present blocks (such as D) which will
interrupt the fall that would have been predicted by a theoretical
physicist from equations and measurements describing A and B.
As in this case, many detailed relations between blocks are
implicit in the diagrammatic representation which could be
explicitly stated only with the greatest difficulty. To take another
example of this advantage of the diagrammatic representation,
consider the recognition of empty space. What space is initially
empty, and what would remain empty after stabilization of the
blocks, can be directly discovered from the diagram and the
imagined snapshots. But previous "blocks-world" programs
have had to rely on highly counterintuitive assumptions about
empty space, and/or have had to make complex mathematical or
logical calculations to *deduce* the empty space in the scene.

Funt's work is relevant to the topic of naive physics discussed
earlier. He points out that the physical knowledge exploited by
his system is comparable to that of the lay person rather than the
physicist. Thus the system has simple computational procedures, or "perceptual primitives", which address the visual array
in parallel so as to identify area, centre, point of contact, symme-
try, and so on. These spatial notions are likely to be useful in
many different problem domains. Also, the program has knowl-

edge of *qualitative* physical principles relevant to its actual tasks, such as that if an object sticks out too far it will fall, and that it will pivot around the support point nearest to the centre of gravity. Moreover, since it is able to discover the empty space, and also those spaces that would remain empty throughout stabilization changes, it possesses a type of knowledge that would be crucial to an animal looking for a pathway or for a safe space through which to move. Leaping animals, at least those whose weight might cause significant changes in the terrain leapt upon, presumably have some understanding of support and of potentially dangerous or unstable structure. For instance, chameleons clambering in trees seem to be capable of making a number of these judgements, preferring thick branches to thin ones and avoiding blind ends or gaps. Experimental study might help show what types of instability various animals are able to recognize, and perhaps whether they are able to distinguish any class of scenes as the likely outcome of a specific sort of instability. Are they able, for example, to distinguish between unstable structures differentially likely to collapse onto a baby animal underneath?

Funt has shown that Sloman's distinction between types of representation can be exemplified in computational terms, but much as Sloman's work is suggestive rather than definitive, so Funt's work is exploratory only. Among its specific limitations, Funt mentions its total ignorance of velocities, acceleration, and momentum. He remarks that were these matters to be included in a future version of the program (which of course would enable types of prediction currently impossible to it), they would have to be represented in terms of equations. But it is not obvious that some useful qualitative distinction between *fast* and *slow* might not be available to some creatures incapable of formulating equations. Ethological evidence is in principle relevant to this question, but so also would be an abstract understanding of the computational power of Fregean and analogical representations. If principled results were to be arrived at within computational logic, expressing the advantages and disadvantages of these representational modes, we might be better able to understand the cognitive potential available at different points in the phylogenetic scale.

Objections: Validations, Parallelism, and Phenomenology

The *Punch* cartoonist obviously recognized that, from the fact that *if* the kingfisher were consciously applying Snell's law its dives would be (as they are) appropriately placed, it does not follow that this is indeed the explanation of its diving ability. Analogously, if one had produced a computational model whose performance mapped onto the kingfisher's behaviour one could not thereby be certain of having captured the bird's psychology. For, as is often pointed out by critics of cognitive psychology [Heil, 1981], there is always in principle more than one model capable of matching observed behaviour. However, this caveat is a special case of the general truth that *any* scientific theory is necessarily underdetermined by the evidence. That this undetermination causes methodological problems is well-known to every practising scientist. Someone offering computational theories of animal behaviour would be no worse off on this account than any other psychologist faced with the task of testing theory against data.

The special difficulty is not how to choose between several alternative computational accounts, once we have got them, but how to arrive even at *one* in the first place. Psychologists and philosophers unfamiliar with AI typically underestimate the procedural-representational complexity of human and animal minds, and may not even realize that there are unsolved computational problems related to everyday psychological descriptions. That is, descriptions of perception and action are assumed to be unproblematic which in fact are deeply puzzling. Thus more ethologists take the existence of various interpretative and representational capacities for granted, and concentrate on asking which of these capacities are shared by which species. Theorists sympathetic to AI, by contrast, are primarily interested in how such capacities are computationally possible.

For instance, the experimental psychologists Premack and Rumbaugh [1978; cf. Savage-Rumbaugh, Rumbaugh, & Boysen, 1978] have asked *whether* chimps can perceive the world as humans can, and do things which we can do. Can a chimp perceive a movie as representing a second individual trying to solve a problem, like reaching bananas or switching-on a heater? Can a chimp plan ahead of time, either on its own behalf or on behalf of its fellow? Can two chimps cooperate in the solution of a task, perhaps using artificial symbols as publicly observable indicators of the tool that is required at a given stage of the problem?

Computationally-inclined psychologists or epistemologists, however, are more likely to be interested in *how* these things can be done, irrespective of which species mange to do them. How is it possible for a creature to perceive intentions, or to ascribe specific beliefs and difficulties to another individual? How is it possible for a creature to form means-end plans for reaching a desired object, plans within which other objects are represented as instruments to the overall end? How is it possible for an external symbol, as well as one in the internal representational medium of the creature's mind, to be employed by one animal and perceived by another as a request for a specific tool? How is it possible for a creature to perceive apparent movement, or to distinguish visually between replacement, motion, and change?

It is this difference in theoretical focus which has led Sloman [1978b] (whose work on analogical representation was mentioned above) to acknowledge the fascination of these recent studies of chimps, and yet to complain that such studies are premature: "In the long run we shall all learn more if we spend a little less time collecting new curiosities and a little more time pondering the deeper questions. The best method I know of is to explore attempts to design *working* systems [i.e., programs] that display the abilities we are trying to understand. Later, when we have a better idea of what the important theoretical problems are, we'll need to supplement this kind of research with more empirical studies."

Ethologists may reply that they wish to discover *which* achievements are within the grasp of chimps, beavers, and bees. This is indeed a legitimate question: natural history should include comparative psychology, an account of what different animal species can do. Many such question have remained unasked by professional ethologists, because of the inhibitory influence of behaviourism—and even of the founding fathers of ethology, who were anxious to avoid sentimental anthropomorphism. But it remains true that a deeper understanding of animals' minds will require careful attention to the computational processes underlying their observed abilities.

However, perhaps there is a particular reason (over and above the *a priori* possibility of alternative theoretical models) for denying the relevance of AI ideas to animal psychology? Even in the human case, it may be said [Dreyfus, 1972], it is doubtful whether computations like those used in AI go on (except possibly during conscious logical or mathematical calculation). And animal minds, *a fortiori*, do not engage in this sort of computation (which is why the *Punch* cartoon would have been less funny if it had shown a human fisherman). Introspection does not reveal complex sequences of step-by-step formal reasoning. If anything, it suggests that many unformulated ideas influence our experience simultaneously. Perception in particular seems relatively immediate, and the notion that a bird's perceptions are laboriously constructed by strings of formal computations is absurd. What is more, the vertebrate brain appears to be capable of parallel processing, so programs written for digital computers are of questionable relevance to human or animal psychology. In short, the complexity of thought may be less than is assumed by AI-workers—and, moreover, may be of a very different type.

This objection is, in part, an appeal to ignorance. From the fact that a mental process does not appear in introspection one cannot infer that it does not go on at non-conscious levels of the mind. What is more, there is a great deal of empirical evidence (amassed over many years) suggesting that human perception is the result of a non-introspectible process of construction, a process that takes a measurable amount of time and that can be interfered with in specific ways. One might, of course, argue that all talk of non-conscious mental processes is so philosophically problematic as to outlaw cognitive psychology in general (irrespective of whether it uses AI-ideas) [Malcolm, 1971]. This extreme viewpoint would deny to theoretical psychologists rights of extended language-use that other scientists enjoy [Martin, 1973]. Short of this position, one must admit the possibility of non-introspectible mental processes.

But what of the objection that, while such processes probably do exist, they may be very different from the processes posited by AI? The first thing to be said in reply is a familiar Popperian theme: a clearly articulated hypothesis, which fails to match the facts in certain specifiable ways, can be a crucial stage in the development of a more satisfactory scientific understanding. So even if AI were incapable of modelling actual thought-processes, it would not follow that nothing of theoretical interest could have been learned from it. The second point is related to the first: the scientific research-programme that is AI includes a number of significantly different approaches. As the reference above to "parallel processing" suggests, the logical-sequential approach is not the only possible form of a computational model.

Some very early work in AI attempted to model parallel processing, but the machines available were so primitive that little was learnt from this exercise. Most research in the field has concentrated on modelling logical-sequential computation, which is well suited to general-purpose digital computers. As a corollary, AI-workers have tended to play down the importance of neurophysiological knowledge about the brain. This is partly due to the fact that many significant computational questions can be pursued quite independently of hardware-considerations, but is also due to the fact that a "general-purpose" machine is precisely one whose hardware is capable of carrying out indefinitely many different types of computation. In recent years, however, neurophysiological and psychophysiological evidence has been taken more seriously by some AI researchers. Recent work takes a radically new approach to computation, wherein parallel processing by dedicated (as opposed to general-purpose) hardware is used—or simulated—in computing properties previously assumed to require highly abstract sequential processing.

One such property is shape, and it is pertinent to our topic to note that the perception of shape is being modelled in this way [Hinton, 1981]. On this approach, a shape can be recognized as a whole without the constituent parts being recognized as such (a part is represented in a radically different way if it is seen as a Gestalt in its own right). We saw above that shape-perception is not needed for recognition of object-identity, so that if we were to attribute identity-perception to a creature (perhaps because of its ability to follow a moving target) we would not thereby be justified in attributing shape-perception also. But, if we were to attribute shape-perception to a perceiver, what computational powers would we be crediting the subject with? If shape-perception required the application of high-level concepts, it would be implausible to say, for example, that a kingfisher can see the shape of a stickleback (which I described earlier as "a sort of narrow pointed ellipse with sharp projections on its upper surface", and which we could describe in many other ways). But this very recent AI work suggests that the bird might be able to perceive the shape of a stickleback despite being unable to represent it in terms of high-level concepts. Further, it implies that the kingfisher need not be able to articulate the image of the stickleback into independently recognized component parts: it could perceive a fish without being able to perceive a fin.

A computational model of this type that was initially developed for shape-perception is now being applied to the control of bodily movement [Hinton, 1984]. The bodily skill of smoothly moving one's arm requires delicate compensatory movements in the various joints, as well as subtle control of velocities at different stages of movement. Earlier attempts to compute motorcontrol met with very limited success. For example, roboticists relying on sequential processing were unable to write programs capable of computing the subtly balanced flexions of shoulder, elbow, and wrist that would be necessary for smooth movement of a robot arm. But these aspects of motor-control are now being modelled by these new AI techniques, with encouraging results. Many problems remain; for example, it is not yet known how to compute a path that will avoid an obstacle placed between the arm and the end-point of movement. But these new developments in AI should give pause to those philosophers (including phenomenologists) who complain that AI can have nothing to say about bodily skills, and so is questionably relevant to human and animal forms of life.

But if simultaneous perceptual processing and bodily skills are not wholly intractable to a computational analysis, what of experience itself? Can AI have anything useful to say about consciousness?

I remarked above that von Uexkull's pictures fail to express the phenomenological quality of what it is like to be a sea-urchin, fly, or dog—or, one might add, a bat. Nor would different pictures have succeeded where these failed. As T. Nagel [1974] points out, the problem in understanding what it is like to be a bat rests on the difficulty of matching different subjectivities. Assuming (as we all do) that our experience is somehow intrinsically different from the bat's, how could we even conceive of what the bat's experience is really like—that is to say, what it is like for the bat? No mere subtraction or addition of conceptualizable features could transform our own experience into the bat's.

Related points were made with respect to spatial perception, in the discussion of naive physics above. Since it is implausible to suppose that a creature's understanding of "inside" is independent of its manipulative abilities, a kingfisher's perceptual experience of containment would differ from the chimp's. Similarly, no dog could perceive a bone to be *inside* a box in the same way in which human adults can, because a baby's sensorimotor understanding of spatial concepts is radically transformed (not merely added to) by the learning of language.

This difficulty in understanding different subjectivities casts doubts on the possibility of a theoretical phenomenology, and *a fortiori* seems to dash any hopes of a systematic comparative psychology concerned with the experience of animals. But at the end of his paper Nagel hints at the possibility of an objective phenomenology. Its goal would be to describe (at least in part) the subjective character of experience in a form comprehensible to beings incapable of having those particular experiences. Structural features of perception, he suggests, might be accessible to objective description even though qualitative aspects are not.

Unfortunately, Nagel gives no examples of what might be meant by "structural" features of phenomenology. Could AI ideas help to clarify these suggestive remarks?

Ullman's work is premised on the phenomenological fact that human beings can experience apparent movement in several different ways. From a subjective viewpoint, these differences do not seem to depend on linguistically represented concepts, and moreover are of such a general character that it is implausible to ascribe them uniquely to human perceivers. That is, if a creature's phenomenology has any dimension comparable to visual experience as we know it, we can intelligibly ask whether (and when) distinctions such as these are perceived by it. We can ask, for instance, whether it enjoys any or all of the experiences, "seeing the same thing moving", "seeing one thing being replaced by another", "seeing a thing of a particular shape", and "seeing a thing being transformed into another". Indeed, that such questions are intelligible is largely what is meant by saying that its phenomenology "has a dimension comparable to visual experience as we know it."

The relevance of Ullman's study is that he provides theoretical accounts of differential (human) phenomenology that can be empirically investigated, and which if correct would explain how and why these distinct experiences arise when they do. This account is couched in computational terms, which are objective rather than subjective but which relate to what one might call the "structure" of phenomenology. That is, phenomenological distinctions such as those just listed can be intelligibly related to hypothetical underlying computations (whether Ullman's hypotheses are correct is not of central interest here). Moreover, "structural" relations between them can be clarified, by showing for instance that *this* computation is or is not a necessary prerequisite or accompaniment of *that* one. For example, Ullman's demonstration that computation of identity gives theoretical support to the view that a creature might be able to experience identity without being able to recognize shape. So evidence (whether behavioural or biological) of a creature's ability or inability to perform certain computations could count as theoretical grounds for denying experiences of certain types to it. This is not to identify computation with consciousness. We know from the example of "blindsight" that "visual" computations can occur without any conscious phenomenology [Weiskrantz, 1977]. Nor can one escape the difficulty that Nagel ascribes to all "reductive" theories of the mental, that their truth is logically compatible with the absence of any subjective aspect whatever. But Nagel himself—like biologists and ethologists in general—is content to take for granted that other creatures do have experiences. He does not require of an objective phenomenology that it provide a philosophical proof of this presupposition. Rather, he asks for what one might term a systematic study of the structural constraints on "seeing-as", a study which would illuminate our own subjective life as well as enabling us to say something about the experiences of alien creatures.

Again, Nagel gives no examples to show what sort of study this might be. Possibly relevant are computationally-influenced investigations of visual imagery that have sought to explain introspectively obvious but intuitively mysterious facts about our visual experience. For example, it has been found that some striking perceptual differences in viewing a wire-frame cube (including, for example, the ease with which certain mental images can be formed of it) depend on which alternative structural description of the object is assigned to it by the perceiver [Hinton, 1979]. That is, an object seen as one sort of structure can be experienced (and imagined) in ways different from those made possible by seeing it as another sort of structure. This approach to visual perception illuminates the nature and generation of our own experiences, and could in principle provide theoretical grounds for saying that a bat, or a Martian, who applied a specific (objectively definable) structure description to an object would be more likely to experience a specific type of imagery accordingly.

In sum, computational ideas are in principle relevant to the psychology of animals, and to their phenomenology too. Counter-intuitive though this may seem, AI might help us understand the intelligence and perceptual experience of kingfishers as well as kings.

Chapter 9
Educational Implications of Artificial Intelligence

The well-known reason for climbing Everest—"Because it is there"—may be adequate justification of the mountaineer's obsession, but it would not suffice to explain why people involved in education should be interested in artificial intelligence (AI). AI is the attempt to write programs enabling computers to do the sorts of things that human (and animal) minds can do [Boden, 1987]. Like every human activity, it has its own peculiar fascination. But there are more pressing reasons why AI is educationally relevant, reasons of both a theoretical and a practical kind.

Many cognitive psychologists today look to AI for help in understanding problem-solving, learning, and intelligence. Even creativity might be illuminated by AI-ideas [as argued in Chapter 7 of this volume]. Psychological theory can be expected to influence pedagogical practice, and relevant recommendations have already been drawn from the AI way of thinking about thinking. The entry of AI into the classroom in the form of AI-based automatic tutors calls for an appreciation of the differences between this approach and the traditional view of computer-assisted instruction. Current work with handicapped children suggests that AI-ideas can help them to realize their intellectual and emotional potential. And the increasing use of computers in schools and universities prompts one to ask whether social life will be impoverished by the widespread introduction of "intelligent" programs into educational institutions. For these various reasons, then, educationists might be expected to take an informed interest in AI.

Educational psychology and pedagogical practice alike are unavoidably (if often implicitly) influenced by general psychology. Today, theoretical psychologists increasingly draw on concepts from AI and computer science in asking questions about thinking. According to the computational approach, thinking is a structured interpretative process. In this view, AI agrees with many non-behaviourist psychologists—such as Piaget, for instance. Indeed, AI agrees with Piaget in a number of ways, including the commitment to formalism and cybernetics, and the insight that psychology (being concerned with meaning and symbol manipulation) is semiotic rather than causal. However, Piaget gave only vague answers to his questions about thinking and its development, and also failed to make his questions about these matters sufficiently detailed: his vocabulary of "disturbance", "regulation", and "compensation" is inadequate to express the procedural complexity involved [Boden, 1979; 1982b]. Nor is Piaget alone in this. Non-computational psychologists in general tend to underemphasize mental process, taking it for granted as unproblematic rather than enquiring into it. This is hardly surprising, since computational concepts are needed to express the content, structure, construction, comparison, transformation, function, and development of differing representations and information-processes. A central lesson of AI, then, is that our theoretical aim should be to specify the procedural complexity of thinking.

One way of attempting to do this is to write computer programs that achieve an intellectual task that human thinkers can manage. Because programmed procedures must be explicitly and rigorously defined, this exercise may provide ideas as to what psychological processes might be involved—and it will certainly help to locate lacunae in current psychological theory. However, the way in which a program does something may bear very little relation to the way in which human minds do it. Careful comparisons need to be made between the various levels of the program and psychological data, to assess the degree of match between the artificial and the natural systems. In many cases, the relevant data are not available. Often, there are methodological difficulties in deciding just which aspects of the program one might plausibly expect to be worth empirical testing (some aspects are included merely in order to produce a program which will run, and have no psychological interest). And many psychologists are not sufficiently interested in the activity of programming to want to spend their time in writing complex programs. For these reasons—not to mention a positive commitment to working with human subjects—many psychologists sympathetic to AI do not desert empirical research for the computer console. Rather, they try to plan their experiments with computational questions in mind, their studies being more closely focused on the procedural details of thinking than is usual.

In developmental psychology, for instance, the computational influence has been largely responsible for the increasing interest in microdevelopmental research. This studies the dialectical interplay between action-sequences and changing cognitive representations (theories, models, heuristics, choice-criteria . . .). The emphasis of microdevelopmental studies differs from more traditional approaches in emphasizing the specifics of action, on the assumption that the procedural details of performance (not only its overall structure) give clues to the underlying competence. Admittedly, Piaget (for instance) took seriously details of action which others had ignored as trivialities. But the degree of detail aimed at in microdevelopmental research is greater—and that which would be need to specify an adequate computational theory of these matters is greater still.

For example, a microdevelopmental study of children's learning to balance blocks found that a non-balanced block may at first be ignored as an apparently irrelevant anomaly, and only later be accepted as a genuine counterexample challenging (and prompting improvement of) the child's current theory [Inhelder & Karmiloff-Smith, 1975]. This fact is not predicted, still less explained, by the generalized talk of "accommodation". The experimenters suggested that the time is needed for "consolidation" of any theory—but they did not ask just what consolidation is, and how it is effected. These questions would need to be answered if "consolidation" were accepted within a computational theory of cognitive change [Boden, 1982, a & b].

Again, microdevelopmental work has cast doubt on the common assumption that the classificatory power of 5- and 10-year-olds is very similar [Thornton, 1982]. This view relies on the fact that the *product* of classification may be identical as between these two age-groups, but ignores the fact that the *activity* of sorting is significantly different. The author's experimental design highlights many procedural differences, and she interprets her observations in broadly computational terms. She suggests that children of 10 treat the whole classification as a single unity composed of interrelated classes, that at 5 they proceed as though each class were independent of the others, and that 7-year-olds attend to the relations between classes so as spontaneously to effect the transition by organizing their initially "juxtaposed" procedures into more coherent systems. She admits that the procedural content of concepts like these needs to be clarified if cognitive development is to be understood, and is currently attempting such a clarification with the help of AI-ideas. (With reference to bugs and creativity, one should note that this author takes her work to show that cognitive change need not be failure-driven, a conclusion that is supported by the comparable finding that a child asked to draw maps may spontaneously construct a more powerful map even though the current on has always succeeded [Karmiloff-Smith, 1979].)

The educational potential of AI has been explicitly recognized by a number of workers in the field. One of these is Seymour Papert, an ex-colleague of Piaget who has been deeply influenced by Piaget's ideas about autonomous constructive learning and the epistomological relevance of the structure (not only of knowing but also) of what is known. Papert's ideas are likely to be influential, not least because in November 1981 he was invited by President Mitterand of France to advise on a new Paris computer research centre (with a budget of $20 million a year) devoted to the development of a low-cost pocket-sized computer that will be available on a mass scale throughout the world. Papert [1980] explores the promise of the nascent "computer culture", focussing not on the many uses people will find for computers, but rather on the power of computational environments to affect the way people think and learn—and, crucially, the way they think about themselves.

Papert reminds us that psychological theories of thinking usually affect educational practice not *via* detailed hypotheses but *via* relatively general ideas, and he identifies a number of "powerful ideas" that enable one to think more confidently and effectively. An important example is the notion of "bugs" in thinking. This concept originated in computer programming, wherein one soon discovers the ubiquity of bugs. Bugs are mistakes, but not just any mistakes: a false factual assumption is not a bug, nor is a momentary slip in executing some procedure, nor the choice of a procedure that is wholly inappropriate to the goal. A bug is a precisely definable and relatively systematic erroneous variation of a correct procedure.

Several AI-workers have attempted a classification of bugs. Sussman [1975] distinguished several types in terms of general teleological notions such as goal, brother-goals, and prerequisite; he wrote a self-modifying learning program that diagnosed its bugs so as to criticize and repair its self-programming accordingly. More recently, O'Shea and Young [1978] have analysed a large sample of children's subtraction-errors in terms of the deletion or overgeneral application of individual rules, such as the "borrowing" rule. Brown and VanLehn [1980; Burton, 1982] have also studied subtraction, and their programs "BUGGY" and "DEBUGGY" provide a notation for precisely describing bugs and a diagnostic tool for identifying errors in students' work. They are developing a "generative theory of bugs", a set of formal principles that can be applied to a particular (correct) procedural skill to generate all the bugs actually observed in the data, and no others. They expect their theory to predict the bugs that occur during the learning of arithmetic, algebra, and calculus (and, possibly, operating computer systems or controlling air traffic).

Their central idea is that many bugs are "patches" (a term drawn from computer programming) that arise from the attempt to repair a procedure that has encountered an impasse while solving a particular problem. Various repair heuristics and critics are defined by the theory, and the way in which a repair will be attempted is theoretically independent of the reason why the procedure was incorrect in the first place. This enables the authors to explain the phenomenon of "bug-migration", wherein a subject has a different bug on two tests given only a few days apart. Using their diagnostic system, they find that only certain bugs migrate into each other, and that they seem to travel both ways. For instance, "Stops-Borrow-At-Zero" migrates into "Borrow-Across-Zero", and vice-versa. The hypothesis is that bugs will migrate into each other if (as in this example) they can be derived by different repairs to the same impasse. Repair theory thus makes empirical predictions about the detailed pattern of errors observed when people are learning skills of thinking.

Despite its emphasis on error, "bug" is an optimistic rather than a defeatist notion. For it implies that elements of the correct procedure or skill are already possessed by the thinker, and that what is wrong is a precisely definable error that can be identified and fixed. In this it differs from the broader notions of "anomaly" and "counterexample", the educational value of which has been stressed for instance in the Piagetian tradition [Groen, 1978]. As Papert puts it, the concept of "bug" helps one to think about thinking in "mind-sized bites". These insights led Papert to develop the LOGO programming language (usable even by six-year-olds), in the conviction that AI in the classroom could help children to a fruitful insight into their own thinking-abilities. There is some evidence that the experience of LOGO-programming does indeed encourage children to replace the passively defeatist "I'm no good at this" with the more constructive "How can I make myself better at it?" [Papert, 1980; Howe, O'Shea, & Plane, 1980].

Papert thus stressed the educational value of the activity of programming itself. But AI can enter the classroom in another way, namely, in the form of tutorial programs. Automatic teaching-aids, of a sort, have long been with us. B. F. Skinner's "teaching machines", and their descendents in "computer-assisted instruction" (CAI), can vary their response to a limited degree with the student's level of understanding, by means of branched programs with predefined choice-points. But the flexibility of tutorial programs based in AI is much greater, because they incorporate complex computational models of students' reasoning that enable them to respond in more subtly adaptive ways. A number of such programs already exist that are useful in limited domains, and several groups around the world are working on these issues [Sleeman & Brown, 1982]. Only if clear articulation of the knowledge involved in the chosen domain has been achieved can it be embodied in an instructional programe—though before this embodiment it might be usable by a human teacher in an instructional programme. "DEBUGGY", for instance, is as good as or better than human diagnosticians at discovering the (nearly one hundred) bugs that explain a student's subtraction errors. In the hands of a specially-primed teacher, it can be put to use in the classroom. It has not yet been incorporated within a remedial program, with which students can interact to improve their subtraction skill; nor has it yet been presented in such a form as to be usable as a diagnostic aid by any maths teacher. But these educational developments are in the forefront of the authors' minds, one of Brown's main aims having long been to develop diagnostic and remedial principles that can be used by tutors—whether human or automatic—to help people learn [Brown & Burton, 1975]. (Some practice with DEBUGGY might profitably be provided in teacher-training courses, even though it cannot yet be adopted as a classroom tool.)

The view implicit in DEBUGGY, that special-purpose rules and heuristics are necessary for intelligent problem-solving, is consonant with the view of intelligence now held by many people in AI. In the early days of AI-research, it was a common assumption that very general thinking procedures suffice to solve most problems. This faith was reflected in the title of one of the most famous early programs, the "*General* Problem Solver" [Newell & Simon, 1963], and it motivated much of the early work in "theorem-proving". Since then, it has become increasingly apparent that, while there are some relatively general strategies (such as depth-first or breadth-first search, for instance), the intelligent deployment of knowledge also involves large numbers of domain-specific heuristics suited to the structure of the subject-matter concerned.

Like the notion of "buggy thinking", this view of intelligence contradicts the all-too-common idea that intelligence is a monolithic ability, which one either has or lacks willy-nilly. If more ammunition against so-called "Intelligence Tests" were needed, there is a full arsenal here: the AI approach highlights the absurdity of trying to assess people's intelligence by deliberately *preventing* them from using any of their acquired expertise [Gregory, 1981, pp. 295-333].

Intelligence being the deployment of many special-purpose skills rather than one general-purpose ability, learning and microdevelopment must involve the gradual acquisition of myriad domain-specific facts and heuristics. Many of these are presumably picked up during the initial "immersion" in a problem-domain, when the unskilled person may appear to be merely thrashing-around. Just how they are picked up is, however, obscure. The microdevelopmental studies previously enjoined thus need to focus on precisely what information is being attended to by the child at a given time, and what micro-strategies she is using to deploy it, with what results.

The case for asking these informational questions, with reference to distinct procedural rules, has been argued in the context of an AI-model of children's seriation-behaviour. Young [1976] showed that qualitative behavioural differences can result from the addition or deletion of one simply definable Condition-Action rule. Moreover, the use of a rule once it has been acquired depends on tests related to its appropriateness in a particular informational context. For example, even adults will use a trial-and-error seriation strategy if given a large number of blocks, differing only slightly in length. Piaget explained this in terms of "regression" from the formal to the concrete operational stage, implying that the subject chooses a sub-optimal method over an optimal one. However, the informational demands here differ from those when there are only a few blocks, of obviously differing lengths. The perceptual judgment of which block is the largest (or smallest) cannot now be made "instantly", since the information from so many blocks cannot be handled all at once. Consequently, the optimal informational strategy is to compare the blocks one-by-one. Young's study of seriation is in the microdevelopmental rather than the macrodevelopmental category, not only because he is able to explain minute details of behaviour (such as the stretching out of the hand towards a block that is not then picked up), but because of his AI-based view that intelligent behaviour is better described in terms of many independent rules than in terms of holistic structures.

Handicapped children can benefit greatly from an AI-based computational environment [Weir, 1982, 1987; Weir & Emanuel, 1976]. I have in mind here not the uses of computers as gadgetry (controlling typewriters and the like), practically important though these are. Rather, I am thinking of recent research showing how AI can help encourage a variety of intellectual and emotional abilities. That is, AI can be used not only to study the mind of a handicapped person, but also to liberate and develop it. Weir, a psychiatrist with a mastery of AI techniques, has worked with a number of different handicaps and has started a long-term project with the sponsorship of the MIT School of Education. Commenting on the varied examples she describes, Weir points out that we have as yet only scratched the surface of what is possible.

For example, her work with a severely autistic child suggests that a sense of autonomous control (over oneself and others) may develop for the first time as a result of the experience of interactive (LOGO-) programming. The immediacy of results and the non-human context (in which the threat of personal rejection or adverse judgment is removed) combine to provide an inducement for the emotionally withdrawn child to venture into a world not only of action, but of interaction. Interaction with human beings follows, apparently having been facilitated by the computational experience.

Again, one may wish to build on and improve the spatial intelligence of severely palsied children. Since they lack normal sensorimotor experience, one might expect them to suffer from generalized disabilities of spatial cognition. But manipulative tests are clearly of little value in assessing just what abilities a palsied child has or lacks. The use of computer graphics (for which LOGO was developed) provides a window onto the intelligence of these children, one that allows diagnosis of their specific difficulties in understanding spatial concepts. Weir's aim being not just to understand their minds but to help change them, she has the satisfaction of reporting considerable advances in the children's intellectual achievement and general self-confidence.

Linguistic defects, too, may be bypassed in assessment based on computer graphics. For instance, a grossly dyslexic boy was found by Weir to have a superior spatial intelligence, involving highly developed metaknowledge in the spatial domain. The dissociation between linguistic and spatial knowledge is, of course, consonant with the AI view of intelligence discussed above. Much as I suggested above that "DEBUGGY" might be useful for teacher-training, even though it is not ready for use as a classroom tool, so ideas arising from Weir's LOGO-projects might be put to use in the training of teachers for the handicapped. But since it is a prime claim of her approach that the experience of interaction with a LOGO-machine is itself highly therapeutic, she would recommend increased availability of computers for use by handicapped people.

This raises an aspect of the "computer culture" awaiting our children that has not yet been mentioned, namely, the enormous increase in the number of computers used in society. By 1980 there were already two million personal computers in use in the USA [Levin & Kareev, 1980], and the market is expanding; and there is an increasing use of programs by institutions (governmental, medical, educational, and commercial). In their discussion of "the future with microelectronics", Barron and Curnow [1979] point out that, as well as vocational training and adult retraining, we shall need contextual education to ensure that everyone is aware of the technology and its possible consequences. As users get less expert, there will be an increasingly urgent need for relevant nonspecialist courses in higher education. They conclude that "It should perhaps be a target that every graduate has the capability to use computer systems and a thorough understanding of their potential [and, I would add, of their limitations]" [p. 231].

Several universities are already running courses with these aims in mind, and some people are already doing comparable work with school pupils. For instance, we at the University of Sussex (in the School of Cognitive Sciences) have found that one can alert naive—and non-numerate—users, on their first day of programming experience, to two important facts: that even an "intelligent" program is incapable of doing many things that one might *prima facie* expect it to do, and that even a nonspecialist user may be able to modify the program so as to make it less limited. A conversational or visual program, for example, is initially impressive, but the user soon realizes that apparently "obvious" inferences about the meaning of the input words or pictures are not actually being made by it. The beginner-student can then attempt to supply the missing rule so that the un-made inference can now be drawn. Since they themselves are altering these complex systems, students gain confidence in the activity of programming. More important, they realize that programs, however impressive they may be, are neither godlike nor un-alterable.

These insights would not readily be communicated merely by teaching students to program—in FORTRAN, for example, or BASIC. They are best conveyed by way of specially prepared teaching-demonstrations making use of AI techniques, which can be run only on powerful computing systems (which, with the rapid advance of hardware-technology, become less expensive every year) [Sloman, 1984b]. (Ours owe a great debt to the late Max Clowes, whose imaginative vision of student-friendly computing environments inspired us all [Sloman, 1984a]). Educational projects such as these are socially important, since for most people the ability to write usable programs will be less important than the ability to use—and to avoid misusing—programs written by others. This sort of computer literacy will be necessary if people are to be able to take advantage of this new technology rather than being taken advantage of by it.

Widespread access to computing environments, especially in primary or middle schools, may have social-psychological effects that educationists should think about. The computer-junkie, or "hacker" [Weizenbaum, 1976, pp. 115-126] has already appeared in infantile form—so much so that a brochure for a children's computer-camp reassured parents that their offspring would not be allowed to remain at the terminal all day, that they would be *forced* to ride, swim, or play tennis. Whether this presents a threat to normal social development is not yet known. Research on the impact of such environments on young children's play-patterns is currently being planned [Robert Hughes, National Playing-Fields Association: personal communication], in the hope that any unwelcome changes in play-behaviour which ensue could be forestalled in the future.

One should not assume, however, that any changes in social interaction would necessarily be unwelcome ones. For instance, there is some evidence in the LOGO-projects that the greater self-confidence induced by a child's experience of computing can lead to less anti-social behaviour. Moreover, programming contexts are in some ways less oppressive than interpersonal ones, and so have a liberating potential that could be useful in education. This potential has already been mentioned with respect to the autistic child who was led to interact with people after the safer experimentation in a computational environment (and it has been observed also in the context of medical interviewing [Card *et al.*, 1974]). A computer system is something to which (not to whom) one can direct remarks that do not carry their usual social consequences [Pateman, 1981]. Interaction with the system thus avoids the sort of face-saving manoeuvres which, in interpersonal contexts, can inhibit the creative exploration of ideas: "I wonder what it will do if I say this?" is significantly less threatening than "I wonder what she will think of me if I say that?"

In sum, AI has much to offer to people involved in the theory or practice of education. It can help both in the understanding and the improvement of thinking. Through its influence on cognitive and developmental psychology, AI promises to deepen our insight into the procedural complexities of thought. Through its applications in the classroom, AI's view of intelligence as a self-corrective constructive activity can help foster personal autonomy and self-confidence. This is so with respect to normal and handicapped students, children and adults. Used as the basis of intelligent tutorial programs, AI can offer greater aid and challenge to both student and teacher than the more familiar forms of computer-assisted instruction. Last but not least, AI-ideas can be used to convey a deeper understanding of the potential and limitations of programs, in societies where computer literacy will be an increasingly important aspect of the communal good. The satisfactions of viewing AI are not those of scaling Everest. But AI, too, is there: let us not fail to explore it.

References

Ackley, D.H., G.E. Hinton, & T. J. Sejnowski. [1985] A Learning Algorithm for Boltzmann Machines. *Cognitive Science,* 9, 147-169.

Anscombe, G.E.M. [1965] The Intentionality of Sensation. In R.J. Butler (ed.), *Analytic Philosophy II.* Oxford: Blackwell. Pp. 158-180.

Arbib, M. [1969] Self-Producing Automata — Some Implications for Theoretical Biology. In C.H. Waddington (ed.), *Towards a Theoretical Biology, Vol. 2.* Edinburgh: Edinburgh University Press. Pp. 204-226.

Barron, R. & I. Curnow. [1979] *The Future With Microelectronics: Forecasting the Effects of Information Technology.* Milton Keynes: Open University Press.

Barrow, H.G. [1987] Learning Receptive Fields. *Proc. First International Conference on Neural Networks,* Institute of Electrical and Electronic Engineers

Bernheim, H. [1886] *De La Suggestion et ses Applications a Therapeutique.*

Bobrow, D.G. (ed.). [1985] *Qualitative Reasoning About Physical Systems.* Cambridge, Mass.: MIT Press.

Boden, M.A. [1962] The Paradox of Explanation. *Proc. Aristotelian Society, N.S.,* LXII, 159-178. Reprinted in M.A. Boden, *Minds and Mechanisms. Philosophical Psychology and Computational Models.* Ithaca, N.Y.: Cornell University Press, 1981. Pp. 113-129.

Boden, M.A. [1969] Machine Perception. *Philosophical Quarterly,* 19, 33-45.

Boden, M.A. [1970] Intentionality and Physical Systems. *Philosophy of Science,* 37, 200-214. (This volume: Chapter 5).

Boden, M.A. [1972] *Purposive Explanation in Psychology.* Cambridge, Mass.: Harvard University Press.

Boden, M.A. [1979] *Piaget.* London: Fontana.

Boden, M.A. [1981a] *Minds and Mechanisms: Philosophical Psychology and Computational Models.* Ithaca, N.Y.: Cornell University Press.

Boden, M.A. [1981b] The Case for a Cognitive Biology. In M.A. Boden, *Minds and Mechanisms: Philosophical Psychology and Computational Models.* Ithaca, N.Y.: Cornell University Press, 1981. Pp. 89-112.

Boden, M.A. [1982a] Chalk and Cheese in Cognitive Science: The Case for Intercontinental Interdisciplinarity. *Cahiers de la Fondation Archives Jean Piaget,* No. 2-3, 29-46.

Boden, M.A. [1982b] Is Equilibration Important? — A View from Artificial Intelligence. *British Journal of Psychology,* 73, 165-173. (This volume: the larger part of Chapter 7).

Boden, M.A. [1984] Failure is Not the Spur. In O.G. Selfridge, M.A. Arbib, & E.L. Rissland (eds.), *Adaptive Control in Ill-Defined Systems*. New York: Plenum. Pp. 305-316. (Partially included in this volume: Chapter 7).

Boden, M.A. [1987] *Artificial Intelligence and Natural Man*. (2nd edn., expanded). London: MIT Press; New York: Harper & Row (Basic Books). (First edition, 1977.)

Brentano, F. [1874] *Psychologie vom Empirischen Standpunkt*. Partial translation in R.M. Chisholm (ed.), *Realism and the Background of Phenomenology*. Glencoe, Illinois: Free Press, 1960. Pp. 39-61.

Brown, J.S. & R.R. Burton. [1975] Multiple Representations of Knowledge for Tutorial Reasoning. In D.G. Bobrow & A. Collins (eds.), *Representation and Understanding: Studies in Cognitive Science*. New York: Academic Press. Pp. 311-350.

Brown, J.S. & K. Vanlehn. [1980] Repair Theory: A Generative Theory of Bugs in Procedural Skills. *Cognitive Science*, 4, 379-426.

Bruner, J.S. [1959] Inhelder and Piaget's "The Growth of Logical Thinking". *British Journal of Psychology*, 50, p. 365.

Burns, B.D. [1968] *The Uncertain Nervous System*. London: Edward Arnold.

Burton, R.R. [1982] Diagnosing Bugs in a Simple Procedural Skill. In D. Sleeman & J.S. Brown (eds.), *Intelligent Tutoring Systems*. London: Academic Press. Pp. 157-184.

Card, W.I., M. Nicholson, G.P. Crean, G. Watkinson, C.R. Evans, J. Wilson, & D. Russell. [1974] A Comparison of Doctor and Computer Interrogation of Patients. *International Journal of Bio-Medical Computing*, 5, 175-187.

Charcot, J. [1890] *Oeuvres Completes* (Vol. 9).

Charniak, E., & D. McDermott. [1984] *Introduction to Artificial Intelligence*. Reading, Mass.: Addison-Wesley.

Chisholm, R.M. [1957] *Perceiving: A Philosophical Study*. Ithaca, N.Y.: Cornell University Press.

Chisholm, R.M. [1963] Notes on the Logic of Believing. *Philosophical & Phenomenological Research*, 24, 195-201.

Chisholm, R.M. [1963] Intentionality. In P. Edwards (ed.). *The Encyclopedia of Philosophy, Vol. IV*. New York: Macmillan. Pp. 201-204.

Chomsky, N.M. [1959] Review of Skinner's "Verbal Behavior." *Language*, 35, 26-58.

Cioffi, F. [1970] Freud and the Idea of a Pseudo-Science. In R. Borger & F. Cioffi (eds.), *Explanation in the Behavioural Sciences*. London: Cambridge University Press. Pp. 471-499.

Cohen, L.J. [1968] Criteria of Intensionality. *Proc. Aristotelian Society*, 42, 123-142.

Colby, K.M. [1965] Computer Simulation of Neurotic Processes. In. R.W. Stacy & B.D. Waxman (eds.), *Computers in Biomedical Research, Vol. I*. New York: Academic Press. Pp. 491-503.

Collett, T.S., & M.F. Land. [1978] How Hoverflies Compute Interception Courses. *J. Comparative Physiology*, 125, 191-204.

Craik, K.J.W. [1943] *The Nature of Explanation*. Cambridge: Cambridge University Press.

Davis, R., & J. King. [1977] An Overview of of Production Systems. In E.W. Elcock & D. Michie (eds.), *Machine Intelligence 8*. Chichester: Ellis Horwood. Pp. 300-334.

Dennett, D.C. [1971] Intentional Systems. *Journal of Philosophy*, 68, 87-106. Reprinted in D.C. Dennett, *Brainstorms: Philosophical Essays on Mind and Psychology*. Cambridge, Mass.: MIT Press, 1978. Pp. 3-22.

Dreyfus, H.L. [1972] *What Computers Can't Do: A Critique of Artificial Reason*. New York: Harper & Row.

Dreyfus, S.E., & H.L. Dreyfus. [In press] Towards a Reconciliation of Phenomenology and AI. In D. Partridge & Y.A. Wilks (eds.), *Foundational Issues in Artificial Intelligence*. Cambridge: Cambridge University Press. Pp. 471-499.

Evans, E.F. [1982] Functional Anatomy of the Auditory System: Auditory Cortex. In H.B. Barlow & J.D. Mollon (eds.), *The Senses*. Cambridge: Cambridge University Press. Pp. 297-303.

Evans, E.F., & I.C. Whitfield. [1964] Classification of Unit Response in the Auditory Cortex of the Unanaesthetized and Unrestrained Cat. *Journal of Physiology*, 171, 476.

Eysenck, H.J. [1957] *Sense and Nonsense in Psychology*. Harmondsworth: Penguin.

Fahlmann, S.E.A. [1974] A Planning System for Robot Construction Tasks. *Artificial Intelligence*, 5, 1-50.

Fikes, R.E., P.E. Hart, & N.J. Nilsson. [1972] Learning and Executing Generalized Robot Plans. *Artificial Intelligence*, 3, 251-288.

Fodor, J.A. [1980] Methodological Solipsism Considered as a Research Strategy in Cognitive Psychology. *Behavioral and Brain Sciences*, 3, 63-110. Reprinted in J.A. Fodor, *Representations: Philosophical Essays on the Foundations of Cognitive Science*. Brighton: Harvester Press, 1981. Pp. 225-256.

Funt, B.V. [1980] Problem-Solving with Diagrammatic Representations. *Artificial Intelligence*, 13, 201-230.

Gazdar, G.J.M., E. Klein, G. Pullum, & I. Sag. [1985] *Generalized Phrase Structure Grammar*. Oxford: Blackwell.

Gibson, J.J. [1979] *The Ecological Approach to Visual Perception*. Boston: Houghton Mifflin.

Gregory, R.L. [1966] *Eye and Brain*. London: Weidenfeld & Nicolson. (3rd edn., 1977).

Gregory, R.L. [1968] On How So Little Information Controls So Much Behaviour. *Bionics Research Reports*. Dept. of Machine Intelligence, University of Edinburgh. Reprinted in R.L. Gregory, *Concepts and Mechanisms of Perception*. London: Duckworth, 1974. Pp. 589-601.

Gregory, R.L. [1981] *Mind in Science: A History of Explanation in Psychology and Physics*. London: Weidenfeld & Nicolson.

Griffin, D.R. [1978] Prospects for a Cognitive Ethology. *Behavioral and Brain Sciences*, 1, 527-538.

Groen, G. [1978] The Theoretical Ideas of Piaget and Educational Practice. In P. Suppes (ed.), *The Impact of Research on Education*. Washington: National Academy of Education.

Gross, C.G., C.E. Rocha-Miranda, & D. Bender. [1972] Visual Properties of Neurons in Inferotemporal Cortex of the Macaque. *Journal of Neurophysiology*, 35, 96-111.

Hardy, S.M. [1984] Robot Control Systems. In T. O'Shea & M. Eisenstadt (eds.), *Artificial Intelligence: Tools, Techniques, Applications*. London: Harper & Row. Pp. 178-191.

Hayes, P.J. [1979] The Naive Physics Manifesto. In D. Michie (ed.), *Expert Systems in the Micro-Electronic Age*. Edinburgh: Edinburgh University Press. Pp. 242-270.

Hayes, P.J. [1985] The Second Naive Physics Manifesto. In J.C. Hobbs & R.C. Moore (eds.), *Formal Theories of the Commonsense World*. Norwood, N.J.: Ablex. Pp. 1-36. Reprinted in R.J. Brachman & H.J. Levesque (eds.), *Readings in Knowledge Representation*. Los Altos, Calif.: Morgan Kaufmann. Pp. 467-486.

Heil, J. [1981] Does Cognitive Psychology Rest on a Mistake? *Mind*, 90, 321-342.

Held. R., & A. Hein. [1963] Movement-Produced Stimulation in the Development of Visually Guided Behaviour. *J. Comp. Physiol. Psychol.*, 56, 872.

Helson, H. [1959] Adaptation-Level Theory. In S. Koch (ed.), *Psychology, A Study of a Science, Vol. I: Sensory, Perceptual, and Physiological Formulations*. New York: McGraw-Hill.

Hess, E.H. [1956] Space Perception in the Chick. *Scientific American*, 195, 71-80.

Hillis, W.D. [1985] *The Connection Machine*. Cambridge, Mass.: MIT Press.

Hinton, G.E. [1979] Some Demonstrations of the Effects of Structural Description in Mental Imagery. *Cognitive Science*, 3, 231-250.

Hinton, G.E. [1981] Shape Representations in Parallel Systems. *Proc. Seventh Int. Joint Conf. Artificial Intelligence*, Vancouver, 1088-1096.

Hinton, G.E. [1984] Parallel Computations for Controlling an Arm. *J. Motor Behaviour*, 16, 171-194.

Hinton, G.E., & J.A. Anderson (eds.). [1981] *Parallel Models of Associative Memory*. Hillsdale, N.J.: Erlbaum.

Hinton, G.E., J.L. McClelland, & D.E. Rumelhart. [1986] Distributed Representations. In D.E. Rumelhart & J.L. McClelland (eds.), *Parallel Distributed Processing: Explorations in the Microstructure of Cognition*. Vol. 1: *Foundations*. Cambridge, MAss.: MIT Press. Pp. 77-109.

Hinton, G.E., & T.J. Sejnowski. [1966] Learning and Relearning in Boltzmann Machines. In D.E. Rumelhart & J.L. McClelland (eds.), *Parallel Distributed Processing: Explorations in the Microstructure of Cognition*. Vol. 1: *Foundations*. Cambridge, Mass.: MIT Press. Pp. 282-317.

Hofstadter, D.R. [1979] *Godel, Escher, Bach: An Eternal Golden Braid*. New York: Basic Books.

Hofstadter, D.R. [1985] Waking Up from the Boolean Dream, Or, Subcognition as Computation. In D.R. Hofstadter, *Metamagical Themas: Questing for the Essence of Mind and Pattern*. New York: Viking. Pp. 631-665.

Holland, J.H., K.J. Holyoak, R.E. Nisbett, & P.R. Thagard. [1986] *Induction: Processes of Inference, Learning, and Discovery*. Cambridge, Mass.: MIT Press.

Howe, J.A.M., T. O'Shea & F. Plane. [1980] Teaching Maths Through LOGO Programming: An Evaluation Study. In R. Lewis & E.D. Tagg (eds.), *Computer Assisted Learning: Scope, Progress, and Limits.* Amsterdam: North-Holland. Pp. 85-102.

Hubel, D.H., & T.N. Wiesel. [1959] Receptive Fields of Single Neurones in the Cat's Striate Cortex. *Journal of Physiology,* 148, 579-591.

Hubel, D.H., & T.N. Wiesel. [1962] Receptive Fields, Binocular Interaction and Functional Architecture in the Cat's Striate Cortex. *Journal of Physiology,* 160, 106-154.

Hyman, A. [1982] *Charles Babbage: Pioneer of the Computer.* Oxford: Oxford University Press.

Inhelder, B., & A. Karmiloff-Smith. [1975] If You Want to Get Ahead, Get a Theory. *Cognition,* 3, 195-212.

James, W. [1890] *Principles of Psychology.* New York: Henry Holt.

Janet, P. [1906] *The Major Systems of Hysteria.*

Karmiloff-Smith, A. [1979] Micro- and Macro-Developmental Changes in Language Acquisition and Other Representational Systems. *Cognitive Science,* 3, 81-118.

Kneale, W. [1968] Intentionality and Intensionality. *Proc. Aristotelian Society, Supplementary Vol.,* 42, 73-90.

Kohler, I. [1962] Experiments with Goggles. *Scientific American,* 206, 62.

Krige, J. [1980] *Science, Revolution, and Discontinuity.* Brighton, Sussex: Harvester.

Kuhn, T.S. [1962] *The Structure of Scientific Revolutions.* Chicago: University of Chicago Press.

Lehrman, D.S. [1955] The Physiological Basis of Parental Feeding Behavior in the Ring Dove (*Streptopilia Risoria*). *Behaviour,* 7, 241-286.

Lehrman, D.S. [1958a] Induction of Broodiness by Participation in Courtship and Nest-Building in the Ring Dove (*Streptopilia Risoria*). *J. Comp. Physiol. Psychol.,* 51, 32-36.

Lehrman, D.S. [1958b] Effect of Female Sex Hormones on Incubation Behavior in the Ring Dove (*Streptopilia Risoria*). *J. Comp. Physiol. Psychol.,* 51, 142-145.

Lenat, D.B. [1977 (a)] The Ubiquity of Discovery. *Artificial Intelligence,* 9, 257-286.

Lenat, D.B. [1977 (b)] Automated Theory Formation in Mathematics. *Proc. Fifth Int. Joint Conf. Artificial Intelligence,* Cambridge, Mass., 833-842.

Lenat, D.B. [1980] *The Heuristics of Nature: The Plausible Mutation of DNA,* Stanford University Computer Science Dept., Report HPP-80-27.

Lettvin, J.Y., H.R. Maturana, W. Pitts, & W.S. McCullough. [1959] What the Frog's Eye Tells the Frog's Brain. *Proc. Inst. Radio Engineers,* 47, 1940-1959.

Lettvin, J.Y., H.R. Maturana, W. Pitts, & W.S. McCullough. [1961] Two Remarks on the Visual System of the Frog. In W.A. Rosenblith (ed.), *Sensory Communication.* Cambridge, Mass.: MIT Press. Pp. 757-776.

Levin, J.A. & Kareev, Y. [1980] *Personal Computers and Education: The Challenge to Schools.* University of California at San Diego, Chip Report 98.

Lorenz, K. [1937] The Nature of Instinct: The Conception of Instinctive Behaviour. In C.H. Schiller (ed.), *Instinctive Behavior.* New York: International University Press, 1957. Pp. 129-175.

182   References

Lorenz, K. [1977] *Behind the Mirror: A Search for a Natural History of Human Knowledge.* London: Methuen.
McCarthy, J., & P.J. Hayes. [1969] Some Philosophical Problems from the Standpoint of Artificial Intelligence. In B. Meltzer & D. Michie (eds.), *Machine Intelligence 4.* Edinburgh: Edinburgh University Press. Pp. 463-502.
McCulloch, W.S., & W.H. Pitts. [1943] A Logical Calculus of the Ideas Immanent in Nervous Activity. *Bull. Mathematical Biophysics,* 5, 115-133. Reprinted in W.S. McCulloch, *Embodiments of Mind.* Cambridge, Mass.: MIT Press, 1965. Pp. 19-39.
McDougall, W. [1926] *An Outline of Abnormal Psychology.* London: Methuen.
Mackworth, A.K. [1973] Interpreting Pictures of Polyhedral Scenes. *Artificial Intelligence,* 4, 121-138.
Mackworth, A.K. [1983] Constraints, Descriptions, and Domain Mappings in Computational Vision. In O.J. Braddick & A.C. Sleigh (eds.), *Physical and Biological Processing of Images.* New York: Springer-Verlag. Pp. 33-40.
Malcolm, N. [1971] The Myth of Cognitive Processes and Structures. In T. Mischel (ed.), *Cognitive Development and Epistemology.* New York: Academic Press. Pp. 385-392.
Marr, D.C. [1976] Early Processing of Visual Information. *Phil. Trans. Royal Society (London),* 275 (942), 483-524.
Marr, D.C. [1982] *Vision: A Computational Investigation into the Human Representation and Processing of Visual Information.* San Francisco: Freeman.
Martin, M. [1973] Are Cognitive Processes and Structure a Myth? *Analysis,* 33, 83-88.
Mayhew, J.E.W. [1983] Stereopsis. In O.J. Braddick & A.C. Sleigh (eds.), *Physical and Biological Processing of Images.* Berlin: Springer-Verlag. Pp. 204-216.
Mayhew, J.E.W., & J.P. Frisby. [1984] Computer Vision. In T. O'Shea & M. Eisenstadt (eds.), *Artificial Intelligence: Tools, Techniques, Applications.* London: Harper & Row. Pp. 301-357.
Miller, G.A., & P.N. Johnson-Laird. [1976] *Language and Perception.* Cambridge, Mass.: Belknap Press.
Minsky, M.L. [1975] A Framework for Representing Knowledge. In P.H. Winston (ed.), *The Psychology of Computer Vision.* New York: McGraw-Hill. Pp. 211-277.
Minsky, M.L., & S. Papert. [1969] *Perceptrons: An Introduction to Computational Geometry.* Cambridge, Mass.: MIT Press.
Nagel, T. [1974] What is it Like to be a Bat? *Philosophical Review,* 83, 435-451.
Newell, A. [1980] Physical Symbol Systems. *Cognitive Science,* 4, 135-183.
Newell, A., & Simon, H. [1963] GPS — A Program that Simulates Human Thought. In E.A. Feigenbaum & J. Feldman (eds.), *Computers and Thought.* New York: McGraw-Hill. Pp. 279-296.
O'Shea, T., & Young, R.M. [1978] A Production Rules Account of Errors in Children's Subtraction. *Proc. AISB Conference,* Hamburg, 229-237.
Papert, S. [1980] *Mindstorms: Children, Computers, and Powerful Ideas.* Brighton, Sussex: Harvester Press.

Pateman, T. [1981] Communicating With Computer Programs. *Language and Communication*, 1, 3-12.

Perrett, D.I., P.A.J. Smith, D.D. Potter, A.J. Mistlin, A.S. Head, A.D. Milner, & M.A. Jeeves. [1985] Visual Cells in the Temporal Cortex Sensitive to Face View and Gaze Direction. *Phil. Trans. Royal Society London, B.*, 223, 292-317.

Piaget, J. [1958] Equilibration Processes in the Psychobiological Development of the Child. In H.E. Gruber & J.J. Voneche (eds.), *The Essential Piaget*. London: Routledge & Kegan Paul, 1977. Pp. 832-837.

Piaget, J. [1975] Problems of Equilibration. In H.E. Gruber & J.J. Voneche (eds.), *The Essential Piaget*. London: Routledge & Kegan Paul, 1977. Pp. 838-841.

Piaget, J. [1977] *The Development of Thought: Equilibration of Cognitive Structures*. Oxford: Blackwell.

Power, R.J.D. [1979] The Organization of Purposeful Dialogues. *Linguistics*, 17, 107-152.

Premack, D., & G. Woodruff. [1978] Does the Chimpanzee Have a Theory of Mind? *Behavioral and Brain Sciences*, 1, No. 4, 515-526.

Prince, M. [1905] *The Dissocciation of a Personality*. New York: Longmans Green.

Pylyshyn, Z.W. [1984] *Computation and Cognition: Toward a Foundation for Cognitive Science*. Cambridge, Mass.: MIT Press.

Rissland, E. [1978] Understanding Mathematics. *Cognitive Science*, 2, 361-383.

Ritchie, G.D., & F.K. Hanna. [1984] AM: A Case Study in A.I. Methodology. *Artificial Intelligence*, 3, 249-268.

Robinson, G. [1972] How to Tell Your Friends from Machines. *Mind*, N.S., 81, 504-518.

Rock, I., E.S. Tauber, & D.P. Heller. [1966] Perception of Stroboscopic Movement: Evidence for Its Innate Basis (I). *Science*, N.Y., 147, 1050-1052.

Rock, I., E.S. Tauber, & D.P. Heller. [1964] Perception of Stroboscopic Movement: Evidence for Its Innate Basis (II). *Science*, N.Y., 153, 382.

Rosen, C. [1978] *Schoenberg*. London: Fontana.

Rosenblatt, F. [1958] The Perceptron: A Probabilistic Model for Information Storage and Organization in the Brain. *Psychological Review*, 65, 386-407.

Rosenblatt, F. [1962] *Principles of Neurodynamics*. New York: Spartan.

Rumelhart, D.E., & J.L. McClelland (eds.). [1986a] *Parallel Distributed Processing: Explorations in the Microstructure of Cognition*. 2 vols. Cambridge, Mass.: MIT Press.

Rumelhart, D.E., & J.L. McClelland (eds.). [1986b] On Learning the Past Tenses of English Verbs. In D.E. Rumelhart & J.L. McClelland (eds.), *Parallel Distributed Processing: Explorations in the Microstructure of Cognition*. 2 vols. Cambridge, Mass.: MIT Press. Pp. 216-271.

Rumelhart, D.E., P. Smolensky, J.L. McClelland, & G.E. Hinton. [1986] Schemata and Sequential Thought Processes in PDP Models. In D.E. Rumelhart & J.L. McClelland (eds.), *Parallel Distributed Processing: Explorations in the Microstructure of Cognition*. Vol. 2: *Psychological and Biological Models*. Cambridge, Mass.: MIT Press. Pp. 7-57.

Sacerdoti, E.D. [1974] Planning in a Hierarchy of Abstraction Spaces. *Artificial Intelligence*, 5, 115-136.

Samuel, A.L. [1970] Some Studies in Machine Learning Using the Game of Checkers. II:- Recent Progress. In F.J. Crosson (ed.), *Human and Artificial Intelligence*. New York: Appleton-Centruy-Crofts. Pp. 81-116.

Savage-Rumbaugh, E.S., D.M. Rumbaugh, & S. Boysen. [1978] Linguistically Mediated Tool Use and Exchange by Chimpanzee. *Behavioral and Brain Sciences*, 1, No. 4, 539-554.

Schank, R.C., & R.P. Abelson. [1977] *Scripts, Plans, Goals, and Understanding*. Hillsdale, N.J.: Erlbaum.

Searle, J.R. [1969] *Speech Acts: An Essay in the Philosophy of Language*. Cambridge: Cambridge University Press.

Searle, J.R. [1980] Minds, Brains, and Programs. *Behavioral and Brain Sciences*, 3, 417-457.

Searle, J.R. [1983] *Intentionality: An Essay in the Philosophy of Mind*. Cambridge: Cambridge University Press.

Selfridge, O.G. [1959] Pandemonium: A Paradigm for Learning. In D.V. Blake & A.M. Uttley (Eds.), *Proceedings of the Symposium on Mechanization of Thought Processes*. London: H.M. Stationary Office. Pp. 511-529.

Selfridge, O.G. [in press] *Track and Trail in Adaptation*. Cambridge, Mass.: MIT Press.

Sellars, W., & R.M. Chisholm. [1958] Intentionality and the Mental. *Minnesota Studies in the Philosophy of Science*, 2, 507-539.

Sleeman, D.H., & J.S. Brown. [1982] *Intelligent Tutoring Systems*. London: Academic Press.

Sloman, A. [1978a] *The Computer Revolution in Philosophy: Philosophy, Science, and Models of Mind*. Hassocks, Sussex: Harvester Press.

Sloman, A. [1978b] What About Their Internal Languages? *Behavioral and Brain Sciences*, 1, 602-603.

Sloman, A. [1979] The Primacy of Non-Communicative Language. In M. McCafferty & K. Gray (eds.), *The Analysis of Meaning*. London: ASLIB and Brit. Comp. Soc.

Sloman, A. [1980] What Kind of Indirect Process is Visual Perception? *Behavioral and Brain Sciences*, 3, 401-404.

Sloman, A. [1984a] Experiencing Computation: A Tribute to Max Clowes. In M. Yazdani (ed.), *New Horizons in Educational Computing*. Chichester: Elis Horwood. Pp. 207-219.

Sloman, A. [1984b] Beginners Need Powerful Systems. In M. Yazdani (ed.), *New Horizons in Educational Computing*. Chichester: Eliis Horwood. Pp. 220-234.

Sloman, A. [1986a] Reference Without Causal Links. In B. du Boulay and L.J. Steels (eds.), *Seventh European Conference on Artificial Intelligence*. Amsterdam: North Holland. Pp. 369-381.

Sloman, A. [1986b] What Sorts of Machines Can Understand the Symbols They Use? *Proc. Aristotelian Soc., Suppl.*, LX, 61-80.

Smith, B.C. [1982] *Reflection and Semantics in a Procedural Language*. Cambridge, Mass.: MIT Ph.D. Dissertation and Technical Report LCS/TR-272.

Smith, U.K. [1941] The Effect of Partial and Complete Decortication upon the Extinction of Optical Nystagmus. *J. General Psychology*, 25, 3-18.

Smolensky, P. [1987] Connectionist AI, Symbolic AI, and the Brain. *AI Review*, 1, 95-110.

Stein, D. [1985] *Ada: A Life and a Legacy*. Cambridge, Mass.: MIT Press.

Stich, S.C. [1983] *From Folk Psychology to Cognitive Science: The Case Against Belief*. Cambridge, Mass.: MIT Press.

Stratton, G.M. [1896] Some Preliminary Experiments on Vision. *Psychol. Rev.*, 3, 611.

Stratton, G.M. [1897] Vision Without Inversion of the Retinal Image. *Psychol. Rev.*, 4, 341.

Sussman, G.J. [1975] *A Computer Model of Skill Acquisition*. New York: American Elsevier.

Taylor, R. [1966] *Action and Purpose*. New Jersey: Prentice-Hall.

Thornton, S.P. [1982] Challenging "Early Competence": A Process Oriented Analysis of Children's Classifying. *Cognitive Science*, 6, 77-100.

Ullman, S. [1979] *The Interpretation of Visual Motion*. Cambridge, Mass.: MIT Press.

Ullman, S. [1980] Against Direct Perception. *Behavioral and Brain Sciences*, 3, 373-415.

von Holst, E. [1954] Relations Between the Central Nervous System and Peripheral Organs. *Brit. J. Animal Behaviour*, 2, 89-94.

von Uexkull, J. [1934] A Stroll Through the World of Animals and Men. In C.H. Schiller (ed.), *Instinctive Behavior: The Development of a Modern Concept*. New York: International University Press, 1957. Pp. 5-82.

Waltz, D.L. [1975] Understanding Line Drawings of Scenes with Shadows. In P.H. Winston (ed.), *The Psychology of Computer Vision*. New York: McGraw-Hill. Pp. 19-92.

Weir, R. [1962] *Language in the Crib*. The Hague: Mouton.

Weir, S. [1981] LOGO as an Information Prosthetic for Communication and Control. *Proc. Seventh Int. Joint Conf. Artificial Intelligence*, 970-974.

Weir, S. [1987] *Cultivating Minds: A LOGO Casebook*. New York: Harper & Row.

Weir, S. & Emanuel, R. [1976] *Using LOGO to Catalyse Communication in an Autistic Child*. D.A.I. Research Report 15. Dept. A.I., University of Edinburgh.

Weiskrantz, L. [1977] Trying to Bridge Some Neurological Gaps Between Monkey and Man. *Brit. J. Psychol.*, 68, 431-435.

Weizenbaum, J. [1976] *Computer Power and Human Reason: From Judgment to Calculation*. San Francisco: Freeman.

White, R.W. [1959] Motivation Reconsidered: The Concept of Competence. *Psychological Review*, 66, 297-333.

Winston, P.H. [1972] The MIT Robot. In B. Meltzer & D. Michie (eds.), *Machine Intelligence 7*. Edinburgh: Edinburgh University Press. Pp. 431-464.

Winston, P.H. [1975] Learning Structural Descriptions from Examples. In P.H. Winston (ed.), *The Psychology of Computer Vision*. Cambridge, Mass.: MIT Press. Pp. 157-210.

Young, R.M. [1976] *Seriation by Children: An Artificial Intelligence Analysis of a Piagetian Task*. Basel: Birkhauser.

Young, R.M. [1977] *Mixtures of Strategies in Structurally Adaptive Production Systems: Examples from Seriation and Subtraction*. DAI Research Report 33, Dept. AI, Univ. Edinburgh.

Subject Index